RELATIONSHIP
& IDENTITY

OTHER BOOKS BY THE AUTHOR

Revelation: The Birth of a New Age
Festivals in the New Age
The Laws of Manifestation
New Age Rhythms
Links With Space
Anthology: Vision of Findhorn

Findhorn Lecture Series'
Towards A Planetary Vision
Reflections on the Christ

RELATIONSHIP
&IDENTITY

David Spangler

Lecture Series

FINDHORN

Published 1978
Findhorn Publications
The Park
Forres IV36 OTZ
Scotland

Editor
Roy McVicar

Cover Design
Michael Ryan

Cover Photo
Edwin Maynard

Typeset in 10 pt Theme medium
Findhorn Publications

Lithographed and bound in Great Britain by
Biddles of Guildford Ltd.
Martyr Rd.
Guildford, Surrey

ISBN 0 905249 31 3

Introduction

Human life may be seen as a network of relationships. Some of these may be casual and superficial as with one's next door neighbour; others may be profound and intense in their creativity as in marriage. But the quality of these relationships largely determines the quality and happiness of one's personal life and living.

In this book David Spangler explores some of the many dimensions of relationship. It is in no way intended to be either authoritative or exhaustive in its treatment, but rather seeks to clarify some of the essential factors which make up the experience of relationship.

(Note: The masculine pronouns and nouns have been used in their generic sense to include both male and female. Based on lectures given in 1972, the text does not reflect the more recent usage of both masculine and feminine nouns and pronouns.)

Roy McVicar

Most of the following material represents information shared by David Spangler with the Findhorn Community during the years of 1970–1973. As such, it represents a stage in the growth of consciousness of both the community and of David. It was given in response to specific needs or questions existing within Findhorn during those years, and it was intended to be a foundation for further exploration and understanding. In no fashion does it represent a final statement on any of the principles mentioned. It is a particular reflection in time and space of the Universal and has value not only in its particularity but in its use as a guide into that Universal, within which specific words, phrases and teachings must give way to the experience of the truth of Being and Reality. If this material assists you as such a guide, then it fulfils its purpose; it will have taken you beyond itself. If not, then perhaps it may still serve as an indication of where your guide may be by providing you with an experience of where it is not.

Findhorn Publications

Contents

Purity

Man in his true nature is a pure being. Man as a spiritual entity is a pure being. For man is one with God and God is the rhythm of purity.

But man, when he comes to take up his functioning in physical form and takes up expression in the threefold world of body, emotion and mind, becomes impure—not through any sinful cause but by virtue of now having to manifest himself through four distinctly different rhythms of energy.

I say four for simplicity's sake. An occultist could probably divide them up into a number of sub-energies. But man may be looked upon symbolically, and to some extent actually, as a fourfold being. There is the rhythm and energy of his physical nature and its counterpart, the vital etheric body. There is the rhythm and energy of his emotional nature. There is the rhythm and energy of his mental nature. And there is that of his spiritual being.

Purity and synthesis, which is one of the New Age energies, are very much interrelated. If you attempt to bring different qualities, or different energies, or different people, or different ideas together into a synthesis without a necessary purity of consciousness and purity of motive and purity of awareness, what you will end up with is confusion, chaos, compromise. Quite likely you will destroy the synergetic or the together-quality that you are trying to build.

Purity must operate on all levels. In the manuals of spiritual science, yoga, and the training for discipleship in various occult schools, purity of physical form is stressed. This is largely a hold-over from more ancient experiences of the race of humanity when the consciousness was much more concerned with the development and control of the physical vehicle. Purity of physical form is still very useful and for many people a necessary discipline.

The focus of the race now moves not so much towards purifying the physical form as towards purifying the emotional and mental bodies in their interrelationships together. We have, I am sure, all encountered individuals who are very keen on various regimes of physical purity, in fact fanatically so, but who lack a certain quality of emotional and mental sensitivity and awareness and balance. These people may be not really very pleasant or very loving or particularly wise, although physically they may be incredibly pure people.

By the same token it is possible to find individuals who are not following a particularly pure physical regime, yet their emotional relationships with people and with themselves, their emotional relationships with their world and their mental relationships with their world are all quite clear, quite uplifting, quite pure.

If our present civilization fails to meet the test of the times and plunges into the abyss of self-destructiveness, it will not be because we have been physically impure. It will be because we have failed to grasp the necessary combinations of synthesis and purity on emotional and mental levels.

Purity to me means the same thing as clarity. It means the same thing as is expressed in the New Testament: 'If your eye be single your whole being is filled with light.' Purity means the ability

2

and consciousness to sound a clear and distinct note of expression, to manifest a clear and distinct characteristic and quality, to be centred and to know where one is centred, to be clear about one's relationships and about one's destiny. Even though the future may not be terribly clear, one's confidence and attunement to the rhythms of that future can be.

Purity is somewhat synonymous with integration in consciousness. When we talk about a person learning how to be whole, how to blend the physical and emotional and mental and spiritual natures together, we are discussing purity.

A pure being is one who can receive from higher levels the energies of inspiration that exist and resonate on those levels, and translate them accurately into his personality expression. An impure being is one who may be attuned, but is unable to clarify and manifest that attunement through the various levels of his expression. Somewhere along the line it gets distorted. An impure being is one whose emotions tell him to do one thing, and his mind tells him to do something else, and his spirit tells him to do yet a third thing. Somehow he cannot quite get it together.

Purity and rhythm are interrelated. In nature we see a certain purity of expression in such things as the rhythm of the seasons, the rhythm of birth and growth, death and rebirth.

The seventh ray is the ray of synthesis. It is the ray of ordered activity. It is the ray of ceremonial magic. In the past one of the first qualities a magician had to have, whether he was working on the left hand path as a brother of the shadow or on the right hand path as a brother of light, was purity, cleanliness. He could no more enter a magical operation impure than you would walk across a gulf on a rope that was frayed and about to break with your eyes blindfolded and bells ringing in your ears!

One of the ways of purifying a person's consciousness if he is going to do spiritual work is to get down and purify the environment: scrub the walls, scrub the floor, scrub the ceiling,

3

clean it all up and get rid of the dirt. This is absolutely fundamental and elementary to any kind of magical work.

The magic of the seventh ray is soul-magic in its highest aspect and is basically the magic of relationship. In order for this magic to work properly it means that our consciousness must be scrubbed, reasonably purified, reasonably clear and clean like a pool of crystal water, that can allow the light whether it is from God or from the divinity within another being to shine through with certainly a minimum of distortion, preferably with no distortion.

The seventh ray, being the ray of ordered activity, means that it sets into motion those energies within humanity that stimulate group activity and relationship. This ray, this rhythm of energy, is also related to that aspect of consciousness that creates on the physical level. In a human being this means that this energy is related to the generative faculties, the sex faculties.

When this is considered, it becomes apparent that one of the characteristics of seventh ray impact on human consciousness is to stimulate awareness on group levels of the creative power of the group. This can be sexually, emotionally, mentally, spiritually, depending on how the group is oriented. And it can be a blend on all these levels, which is one of the reasons why there exists now in western society a definite consciousness of experimentation where marriage relations and sexual relations are concerned, and a certain movement in experiment towards the concept of group marriage.

Whether or not this represents a definite direction for the future of the race has yet to be seen. It does represent a definite result of seventh ray impact. However if we attempt synthesis without purification first, then we run the risk as does any magician of creating the inverse of what we want. Instead of building and creating wholeness, we will set into motion forces that destroy and that enhance separativeness.

This concept of purity and synthesis in human relations,

particularly in the field of sexual relations and group emotional and mental involvement, is important for all centres where people are coming together under the group-stimulating impulse of New Age energies.

Man as an unintegrated being, an impure being, is like a creature who thirsts. He is seeking that which will quench that need, that thirst. This may be on physical levels, but far more potently now it is on emotional levels and mental levels. True purification, which creates like a pillar of clarity within the being, also creates a tremendous feeling of wholeness, of satisfaction, of togetherness. Impurity on the other hand is just the opposite state.

The way in which the average man seeks to approach this problem is to attempt to define as best he can on what level his need exists, and then to go after it. He may be quite one-pointed in this. For example, I may know clearly that I need a certain kind of emotional expression, that I need someone to express appreciation to me, or someone to express love to me. I may identify my need as a physical one: I need food, I need water, I need rest, I need sexual expression. It may be a mental need: I crave knowledge, I crave information, or something else.

The tendency for man has been to go after that particular need, often to the exclusion of a greater awareness of the totality of his pattern. The result of this is to feed impurity. I may satisfy myself emotionally and leave myself unsatisfied mentally, or vice versa. I can satisfy myself on a personality level, and leave the spiritual level—what Maslow, the psychologist, calls 'meta-needs'—unfulfilled. If that happens I still remain impure and I remain unfulfilled. It does not matter how buried a need is, it still exists. It will continue to act as an irritant within the consciousness.

We say that God's voice is still and small, and in the turmoil of listening to the personality consciousness we may not hear it. Well, his voice may be still and small, but it is rather shrill at the same time. It is a steady note of piercing discontent until it is in some way recognized and its rhythm admitted into the life pattern and fulfilled therein.

Therefore I can gather to myself material things. I can gather to myself emotional successes, prestige, love, friendship. I can gather to myself knowledge and information. And in the middle of all this I still feel unfulfilled. There is still something niggling away on some deep level of consciousness—and so I end up on the psychiatrist's couch! Or I end up on a search, a continual search from one guru to another, from one religion to another, from one town to another, from one possession to another, from one person to another.

Purity, to my mind, refers to the ability of a being to enter into a state of silence, a state of non-activity in the moment, that it can stop and consider what it is experiencing and what it is that is motivating it, and begin to sort out the different levels of motivation and begin to integrate them, so that its actions proceed not from the levels of personality which tends to see things from a rather restricted point of view—whichever point of view is holding the reins in the moment, either the emotions or the mind—but begins to see things from a more total point of view, the embracing point of view of the soul, the rhythm of the inner divinity, and begins to move in such a way that the needs that are met are true needs and they satisfy all levels.

Just as it is said that if a thing is right for one person it will divinely be right for all, it is also true that if a need met is truly right for one level of consciousness, it will enhance all of them. It will enhance the integrative synthesizing process. If this is not the case, then the satisfaction of need on a purely personality level enhances impurity.

This is why through the ages the satisfaction of needs on physical and emotional and mental levels has often been considered sinful. It is not sinful if by that we mean that it puts us in jeopardy with the great workings of the universe and may potentially consign us to an eternity of fire; but it is sinful if by that we mean that it in some way creates a state of non-integration and hence ignorance within our own being.

As the group stimulation develops and people come together and seek to work and live and play and grow together, there is going to be a natural tendency for individuals in the group to see other individuals in the group as potential sources of satisfaction and answers for needs which they are feeling. This may be a good situation. It may be a valid kind of relationship. On the other hand it may be one that is essentially impure because it does nothing to change the rhythm of that person's consciousness. It does nothing to alter the behaviour pattern in a fundamental way that lifts the behaviour pattern towards a new awareness, greater light, greater wisdom, greater love.

One of the challenges to be met by a group that is attempting to implement the New Age energies is literally the challenge to the family structure. Within a family structure we have a state in which not only is one person attempting to become pure, integrated within himself or herself, we also have a state where two people are attempting to create a focus of that purity together and thereby help each other to do it individually.

A fantastic service and definitely one of the paths to divinity! The path of the householder is a noble path. Several of the masters of the Hierarchy are married and have families and serve the race in that fashion. So there is nothing in the spiritual by-laws that says that family life is fundamentally antagonistic to the spiritual life.

As the group develops, however, a situation is created in which a larger family, a larger pattern of purity is seeking unfoldment. As the love is generated, as various energies are stimulated, the family structure comes under natural and perhaps inevitable assault. It takes a very clear strong consciousness to be able to blend the two. But this is good. As that consciousness develops that kind of clarity, that kind of strength, it becomes more pure, more attuned. One of the worst kinds of energy to encounter emotionally is that of frustrated desire. I am sure that it is going to be one of the energies that New Age groups will have to learn to deal with and to purify before they can progress very far. This is a situation in which people are looking in each other for answers to needs.

For example, two people may be married and they married under the conditions of a consciousness in which they saw in each other an answer to a need. But within the context of the greater group one may become aware that his or her needs are not being fully met, and that someone else or some other ones in the group could meet those needs. So there is a pull. At the same time there is a pull to maintain the family in its integrity and its purity. A true challenge for the consciousness!

If it is not properly met, a strange condition arises out of the seventh ray energies in which the ideal of the potential group marriage is brought down into simply promiscuity and group playing around and its inevitable movement towards greater separativeness and lack of wholeness rather than towards the integration that could have been possible.

In a situation of this nature an individual caught with conflicting energies and unable to resolve them must meet another individual in much the same way as two ships passing in the night: a moment's encounter before the need, the basic need, of the fundamental impurity reasserts itself, and sends the individual off on yet another search to find it in the company of another person and another person and another person.

It requires a kind of clear, selfless, and in fact courageous approach to the emotional and mental levels, and certainly to the physical levels of the individual, for this to be dealt with successfully in a group. It can be dealt with quite naturally by the imposition of various rules and regulations. But that is not the New Age approach. Purification is something which is only rarely imposed from the outside. Ultimately the fires that purify must arise from the heart and mind, the soul and the awareness of the individual.

It is far better for a group, whether it is established or still developing, to meet the challenges, whether it is this particular one or some other; and there are many that a group may have to face through individual effort to become the embodiment of the pure state, the clear knowing integrated state.

It is always easy in the moment to give in to the impulse of the moment. Some people define this as freedom. But the moment is the mother of many impulses which are born out of the cradle of mass stimuli. A person who responds only to the moment and to what the moment presents, without being a pure being, is literally a puppet on a multitude of strings. And that is not freedom, even though the puppet may dangle loosely and jerk and jump in a number of apparently free movements.

The individual who has the ability to say 'no' and 'yes' through his own integrated vision is free: this is what my heart tells me and this is what my mind tells me and this is what my soul tells me, and because I am more concerned with the fact that I become a whole being than I am with the satisfaction of need in the moment, I can take the time to listen to this and evaluate it, look at it.

Somehow there is a certain fear that if we do not respond to life spontaneously through our feelings, we shall lose something of the richness of life. But any richness we lose on that level is more than amply replaced by a greater richness that comes from the soul level. This was beautifully portrayed by the Buddha in his discourses on the four noble truths and the eightfold path, in which he said that the being who is simply a wanderer after sensation—sensation and physical form—is a being who is wide open to suffering; and he will continue to suffer because nothing in those realms can satisfy the basic hunger for purity of the being. As already stated, man is essentially a pure being and he will work

9

within himself to manifest that purity.

People often ask by what technique this can be done. How is this purification achieved? Since I am not oriented towards techniques, the best answer I have come up with so far is that within each of us the soul itself is working very diligently to bring about this purification, and it is using life as its greatest ally. If we can be open to the rhythms of experience, we can take time to listen within. This implies some kind of meditative awareness, some entering into silence. If we can take time not to act through pure impulse but to give time for pure inituition to develop, which is every bit as fast and certainly a great deal more accurate—but the two are difficult to distinguish until we have learned how not to act—then we learn again how to act properly.

Through these means, through becoming open and willing to be taught, the teaching will come, the technique will unfold through the very rhythm of one's life. Everything about us is potential fuel for the fires of purification; and just as the magician always had to purify himself before he embarked upon any ritual, so mankind in its collective consciousness is undergoing now purification before it can embark on its next evolutionary sequence as a creative magician, a master of the science of the world and of the forces that create the world.

Purity is not really related to a physical thing. Some people, for example, feel that celibacy is purity. But sex is purity as well. Dirt is purity. The fantastic and ancient image of the lotus growing out of the mud is a symbol of the essential purity of all things when all things are allowed to relate and interrelate together in a synergetic or a mutually beneficial fashion, and separate units are not pursuing their separate course at the expense of the whole.

This, of course, is where we see impurity. In a group it is where individuals pursue their needs without sufficient awareness to see how that pursuit will affect others, especially others with whom he or she may be closely connected.

To move into the New Age requires a strength and a level and a dedication of consciousness beyond what is normally the average manifestation. So moving into the New Age is hard work. And because many people do not relish the idea of hard work they prefer to think of the New Age as something that is being ushered in by cataclysms and flying saucers and gurus and prophets and things like that. All of which may have their part to play but do not replace the essential necessity for individual labour within the furnaces.

Yet the soul of purity is the same thing as the soul of laughter and of joy and of song. Imagine how marvellous it feels when you emerge from a refreshing shower or from a bath or from a dip in the ocean. Imagine how marvellous it feels when you have just heard a beautiful melody played. Imagine how glorious it is when you have just tasted something that resonates so deliciously upon your taste buds, or when you have encountered the fragrance of a flower that tingles and bubbles through your nostrils. Then you have some idea of what purity really is.

Purity is not suffering and asceticism and discipline and denial. Purity is release. It is dropping the burden. It is saying, 'Oh, thank God the quest is over. I am home. I do not have to look in that place and in that person and in that situation for my fulfilment. It is here. It is within me. I am whole. I can give, I can move out to share that with someone else.'

Purity is the kind of release that comes after a hard day of tramping through the hills with a thirty pound knapsack on your back and then you let it down. You breathe in that fresh clear air and you think, 'O God but I am tired! But it sure feels great to get that weight off my back and to breathe that air.' Then you plunge into a mountain stream and you become refreshed.

Purity is life. It is love. It is upliftment. That is why man seeks it so much. That is why man is agitated and unsatisfied until he finds it. He will remain unsatisfied until he learns where to look, until in this new age he learns within the context of the group how to use the energies of that group and of relationship to reveal the homeland of purity and not simply provide the pastures of promiscuity on many levels. For the physical is only a minor part of that which sends man in scattered dispersion of his energies instead of allowing him to find the centredness that is his home and his peace.

Jesus said it all when he spoke about the living waters and what he represented and of the vitality and the joy of his life. And we can say it too, each of us, simply through a change in our vision readjusting our concept of what purification means and what purity implies. We too can begin to be not just living waters but a living torch that can show the way to others.

If I am to relate to you, and indeed to many, then purity is the elimination of the static which blocks that relatedness in our communication. It is certainly the elimination of the inner static, perhaps through discipline, perhaps through an exercise of that kind of knowing that says: 'All right, I want that, I think I need that, I want that other thing. But by the God that is in me, I am going to stand in the midst of this raging torrent; and I will take the energy that is generated through this tension and through this apparent denial and through this apparent discipline, and I will channel that energy into the best service, the best relatedness, the best communication that I know how to create.'

This is why the path of suffering has had a certain value over the past several thousand years: because out of suffering an energy is produced, if an individual knows how to turn suffering away from self-pity and self-involvement and a martyr complex. (Martyrdom in consciousness is the negation of any spiritual values, because martyrdom is suffering turned in on the self in glamour and glorification for what a person is going through.) If one can avoid that and take the energy of tension and turn it into a one-pointed clear light of knowing, by getting his attention off

12

himself and what he is experiencing and on to something else, then you have learned how to master the fires of purification.

They will no longer burn. They will simply energize. They will illumine and they will uplift. They will make you light like bubbles dancing in the froth of the mountain rapids.

As we move into the new, seek to come to terms with the new energies: energies of synthesis and of coming together, of living together in groups, of working together in groups, of necessarily having to deal with many kinds of people, of being faced with the challenge of our age which is that of communication.

We are also faced with the challenge of clarity and of purification and of purity. I commend this challenge to your consciousness for your consideration, for your meditation, so that out of it you may gain a certain awareness and understanding that will enable you as an individual and the groups in which you may be involved to meet the challenges of the times with that force which truly uplifts and which truly creates that which we want to create, which bypasses the pitfalls of the past and the divisions of our bygone heritage and ushers us back into the homeland that is our destiny.

14

Energy and Direction

There is a fable about a young man who sets forth to accomplish a heroic task. On the way he encountered certain companions, and it was because of them that he was able to fulfil the task that he had set himself.

These companions included a giant who was able to take very long strides, a dwarf who had very big ears and could hear sounds for miles and miles, and some other strange being who had very big eyes and could see for miles and miles.

None of these three individuals were particularly smart. In fact they were all rather stupid. So the young man who was the hero provided the brains of the operation. They all rode on the shoulder of the giant: the one who was the eyes could see, and the one who was the ears could hear, the giant provided the mobility and the young man provided the thinking. As they worked together they were able to accomplish their task.

Man is very much like that. We are a combination of individuals, each of whom is geared to expressing energy or the basic life-stuff of the universe in a different fashion. We think that we are one individual. At a certain point in our evolution we become one individual. But until we reach that point we are actually a number of separate individuals struggling to work

15

together in harmony. The greater the harmony with which these individuals can work, the greater the purity. The less harmony and cooperation and communication there is between these individuals or aspects of ourselves, the more impure the expression is for the human being.

What are these individuals? They are the physical body, the etheric body, the astral or emotional or feeling body, and the mental or the thinking body. Beyond that there is the body of the soul. Let me define what I mean by each of these bodies before we go any further.

Some wit once said that the universe is divided into the people who divide the universe into things and those who do not. For the present I am one of those who divide the universe into two things. The universe is divided into form and non-form or spirit. This is a purely relative definition and as soon as you raise your consciousness to the level of spirit a new definition is required. But for our purpose it suffices.

If we say that there is a dividing line between form and non-form then let us say that the physical body represents the most dense, the most compacted, the least sensitive but in some ways the most highly developed of our form bodies, the most highly developed vehicle built out of spirit or energy.

The etheric body is the next most dense form, and it is considered by most occultists simply an extension of the physical body, or vice versa. The astral body is the next less dense form, the energy being more free to operate as energy rather than as form. The mental body is the next less dense, and again the energy is even more free to act as energy rather than as solid limited form.

Then we come to our dividing line. What I mean by the soul is an ambiguous, arbitrary, vague term which implies all the levels of consciousness that are more akin to pure formless spirit than they are akin to form, limitation, definition. We do not need to be any more precise than that.

16

Let us return to the physical form and begin there. Our scientists tell us that everything in the universe is made up of energy. Everything that we see and taste and touch is really energy in motion, and matter is simply an illusion created by a similarity of vibration.

The physical body is made up of billions of individual life units, each of which has its own intrinsic identity, its own form, and all of these are cooperating more or less effectively to create a community. The spirit of that community, the sum total of that community, the living gestalt of that community, is called the physical elemental.

The purpose of the physical body is twofold: one is to provide a point of contact for spirit in order to have some way of communicating with the physical dimension; the second is to provide a microcosmic universe within which billions of individual lives are undergoing a process of evolution. A very primitive kind of intelligence or consciousness—primitive in one sense but certainly very aware in another sense—is undergoing training. This is the consciousness and intelligence within the cellular structure of your body.

This also provides an opportunity for you as the inhabitant of the body, you as soul, to act as if you were a god. For in reality you are the god-centre for your physical body, just as there is a God who is the centre of all life for the physical Earth, for all levels of the Earth.

The physical body can best be represented as being a body of transportation. It is designed to give you mobility so that you can move from one place to another, and so that you can manipulate energy or energy forms.

The etheric body is the body of vitalization. It serves two purposes as well. The etheric body, in the sense that I am using the word, is the basic point of synthesizing or coordinating energy for that community of beings that makes up your physical form.

17

When the etheric body is removed from the physical and the link is cut, an energy of life is also cut from your physical form. What is that energy of life for human beings? When death occurs for a human being, life still goes on within the body. Depending on what area of tissue we are examining, life may continue for several hours as the individual cells continue to live. So hair grows, nails grow, cells deep in the internal structure of the body continue to live and survive even though the entity that we know as that person has died. They will survive until they die as individual cellular units. So even after death occurs life still remains in the body as a flickering ember.

What is it that we call life? What we call human life is this energy of synthesis, the thing that makes all of these cellular individuals function as a whole, function as a united community rather than functioning as a bunch of individual cells. When that synthesizing element is withdrawn, a definite vitalizing energy leaves the cellular structure and the community disintegrates.

An example of this is found in the animal kingdom. If you destroy the queen of a wasp nest the hive will disintegrate, the worker wasps simply stop functioning and get very dopey. They fall asleep and everything begins to disintegrate. They cease to function as a community. So the etheric body provides the point of contact on the physical level where energy from the soul can be spread out to coordinate and to unite all the cellular lives and bind them together as a unity.

The etheric body is also an organ of breathing—not breathing in air but breathing in what is called 'prana' or the basic vital life-stuff, or life energy, that operates on physical levels. The etheric body absorbs this and so provides this life-synthesizing energy. It vitalizes you. When the etheric body is removed at death, and that is what death for human beings actually is, technically, then the body can no longer absorb this 'prana' and it is therefore occultly dead.

18

The astral body functions with energy that is operating on a much more rapid level of vibration. The astral body is a body of gravity. It is a body of attraction. The basic characteristic of the energy that manifests and creates what we call the emotional body is that it is born from the law of attraction and repulsion. The basic quality of the feeling nature, on its most primitive level, is to say: 'I like it, therefore I want it,' or to say: 'I do not like it, therefore I do not want it.' It is either an energy of moving towards or an energy of moving away from; but it is essentially an energy of motion. And motion is a basic creative force. Motion creates relationships. It sets things going.

Therefore the astral body is the body of energy generation for you on the level of form. It will motivate you. It will energize you.

The mental body operates with a different kind of characteristic. It manifests the characteristic of image-producing and of definition and of formation. The mental body on its concrete levels, and even the abstract mind, deals with the ability to create images or forms, through which energy can flow and into which energy can pour and be harnessed. So the mental body to a great extent is the body of direction.

All the bodies of form have one thing in common, but the emotional and mental bodies have this characteristic more powerfully than does the physical: and this is the characteristic of identifying outward. These bodies tend to discover their identity outside themselves. They identify with objects. The emotional body, for example, identifies itself through the law of attraction or repulsion with something in the environment, or something happening within itself in response to the environment. So it generates a feeling of 'I am happy, I am sad, I desire or I do not desire.' The mental body also tends to identify itself with things on the outside.

The level of consciousness that is the first level which can truly identify itself as being the centre is the soul.

The soul and all the higher levels beyond it represent the body of centring, of true identity. It is the first level on which we can say with any truth, 'I am.'

That level, the spiritual level, is where the sense of identity comes from, the true sense of identity. The other levels also have a sense of identity but it is not the true one. They identify themselves with objects, with things in the environment, with other forms of energy, and therefore create certain illusions which man has to deal with.

All bodies, all vehicles, have certain needs and certain motivations, and each of our different bodies are no exception to this rule. It is also true that all forms of energy are living intelligences, are actually entities of some kind or other, and each of our bodies is again not an exception to this rule. What this means is that your physical form and its etheric counterpart— because those two are usually considered together as a closely interrelated pair—have an intrinsic intelligence and livingness and an awareness of certain needs and that intelligence will seek out the satisfaction to those needs.

The astral body has a certain awareness and motivation and it will seek to follow that pattern. The mental body is similar and it will seek to follow its own pattern. We call this intelligence inherent in the energy of each of these bodies the elemental quality of those bodies. So we speak esoterically of the physical elemental, the astral elemental, the mental elemental.

Probably ninety five percent of what we call the spiritual path is composed of learning how to identify oneself with the soul in such a way that the soul takes control over these elementals and in essence absorbs them or disperses them or destroys them, so that you are not four or five different beings, struggling to work together but part of the time moving off in different directions: the astral elemental wanting this, and the physical elemental wanting that, and the mental elemental wanting something else. But you are one being, purely. You move with that singleness of identity, and that is a source of incredible in fact, total—creative power.

Let us again begin at the lowest level and consider the energy of the physical form. Here we are dealing with energy in its most restricted state. It has been encased in form. My physical body can only reach within the radius of my hands and feet. That is not at all true of my emotional body or my mental body, for they can reach several feet, perhaps several yards, perhaps several hundreds of yards, beyond my being. Beyond that they can be projected in a way that is not at all bound by time or space. The energy on these levels is much freer. But here it is restricted in the physical form.

The physical elemental is in itself part of the elemental energy that is part of all physical life patterns. Which is another way of saying that on the levels of form—of body, of feeling and of mind—we are all part of a group soul to some extent or another. Many of the instincts that a person feels do not necessarily arise from that person's identity, but they may arise because they are a part of a current moving through the group identity, the group soul, the elemental currents moving throughout the planet as they are stimulated by a number of forces, planetary or cosmic.

This is one reason why, on certain levels, astrology and numerology can be fairly accurate, because certain vast generalized planetary and cosmic currents can be analyzed and determined. If a person is not operating from the centre of his own identity, he is far more likely to move in rhythm with the currents that are flowing through the planetary ocean of consciousness.

This is true for all needs: whether it is hunger or fatigue, or a need for sexual expression, or whether it is on emotional and mental levels a need for peace, a feeling of anxiety or fear, a feeling of wanting to learn certain things. These can come from

21

individual states but they can also come from mass state, from the currents flowing through mass consciousness. A person really has no way of knowing where it is coming from until they begin to practice disciplines of self-awareness.

If you move into a group where the etheric energy level is rather low, or there are certain draining qualities in the group, you can find that your etheric body is essentially sucked of energy and you will come out of the group feeling, 'Wow! What hit me? I'm really washed out.'

There can be positive reasons for this. A person can encounter an energy field that is really too potent. This is one of the reasons why very highly evolved beings from other levels quite often do not directly approach human beings. They approach through intermediaries who vastly step down the energy, because you can lose energy either by stepping into a vacuum or by stepping into a presence that is far too powerful for you from where you are at that moment. The energy differential is such that a state equivalent to a vacuum is created.

People can have very spiritual experiences but feel tremendously exhausted afterwards and wonder, 'If I have been in the presence of a being or a state that was highly uplifting, why am I not uplifted? Why am I so tired?' It may have been a bit more than their bodies could handle at that moment and they have literally worn themselves out trying to cope with the vast increase in energy. But the overall effect will be good.

If we understand that these mass currents are moving, then we can deal with them. But we need to understand that the elemental consciousnesses of our being will tend to go with the herd.

In the days of Atlantis and Lemuria, when man was still polarized or still expressing his consciousness primarily through his astral body, the centre from which man worked, the centre which provided a sense of identity for him, was provided by outside agencies. This is still done today. An idea is created and people identify with it: the idea of nationality, the patriotic image—Britannia rules the waves, Yankee Doodle; and the symbolic forms that we create have their existence on the inner realms—the British lion, the Russion bear, the American eagle. One of the reasons why nations tend to create these animal images is because they are tuning in through the images to certain etheric energies symbolized by the animals.

So in the days of Atlantis men found their identity and centre provided for them and they were taught and moved within a mass consciousness. This created a state where men could be definitely controlled and were controlled, and a vast conflict ensued which resulted in the destruction of that civilization.

Out of that developed man's increasing polarization into the realm of mind. This is highly important and represents a signficant event in human history—the stimulation of man's mind.

The stimulation of his mind coincided with, indeed created the stimulation of man's sense of self-identity—a movement away from the periphery of his being and seeing his identity out there somewhere as part of the group, as part of a nation, as part of a cult, towards being more aware of himself.

This in its extreme stages was cultivated through inspiring in the race a motion towards selfishness. Selfishness is a highly creative and necessary stage for evolving consciousness to go through. What happens is that the mind creates images with which it then identifies itself, and through holding that identity it marshals the forces of the astral body into that identity. 'I am David Spangler and David Spangler is a certain kind of being based on memory patterns. I have experienced this and I have experienced that, and all of these experiences make up what I say I am.'

The famous statement of Descartes, 'I think therefore I am' affirms the concept of the mind and the ability to think as being the foundation of identity. In point of fact the true statement should be, 'I am therefore I am.' But a person can only say that when he is identifying himself with his soul.

In the meantime the mind serves a useful bridging function because it provides a chance for the person to identify himself with something that is subjective. But this too is an illusion because what we identify ourselves with is still only another form.

The mind draws heavily upon the experiences of the past in order to create an identity. The soul does not. The soul *is*.

This is a fundamental area of differentiation with which human consciousness is now grappling: how to use the wisdom of the past without being conditioned by the past, because the mind will accept conditioning and use it as a means of providing an inner subjective focus of identification. At the same time the mind is not very willing to give up that identification. We are not all that willing to change ourselves—at least we have not been in the past as a race.

While the closed mind, the static mind, the mind that says, 'This is what I am and this is what I have always been and that's it,' has served its purpose in getting man to move inward more and not to be so responsive on emotional levels to things that are happening outside of him, it is now at a point where that kind of attitude that says, 'This is what I am and I cannot change,' is deadly. That is also the attitude that says, 'This is my past and I am doomed to repeat it.' It is also an attitude that can say, 'My creativity is limited to what I have done.'

It is a certain restricted attitude that can deny the abundance of one's spiritual heritage. Nevertheless the mind does provide for the individual the first area of exercising the discipline of 'I am and that is what I am.'

This comes into play in the area of freedom. Men have created laws which are really an outgrowth of the ancient Atlantean and post-Atlantean need for man to have a powerful social structure exterior to himself in order to provide his learning framework. He was not generating it from within himself. He was

24

not self-governing, self-disciplining. So laws are very important, or have been in the history of the race.

But increasingly all through history the concept of freedom comes in—freedom away from external authority, external pressure, external rules and regulations. The reason that kind of freedom was taken away from man initially is because man is far too open to moving with mass currents. Until a person can learn to say, through evaluation of what is best for him, 'No, I will not do this thing. No matter how right it is for other people, no matter how pleasurable it may be to any of my levels, I will not do it if I know that it is not right for me,'—until man can say that, he is vulnerable.

There is a stage in the life experience of each soul where restrictions are removed. He is, as it were, cast out of the father's house and he is told, 'All right, stand on your own two feet for a while.' Sometimes he is faced with a condition in which he is given complete freedom. He has to begin to learn self-discipline, often through very painful experience and a great deal of suffering.

If he does not really make it, then the soul pulls back. It pulls its personality back and the next few lives may see the opposite swing again. He is back into orienting himself towards obedience, towards external authority. After a while he ventures forth again.

Eventually that soul is going to learn the value of using his mind to bring about some kind of order and harmony between the various elemental natures of his being. Instead of simply reacting every time his emotional body says to react, instead of simply moving towards what seems pleasurable, or retreating from what seems non-pleasurable, instead of simply responding to the needs and instincts of the body like eating when you are hungry and sleeping when you are tired, the person goes through various experiences of discipline to learn that the mind is stronger than the emotional and physical levels.

In the life of every soul there comes a time when that person

25

will probably go through a period of yoga, or of celibacy, to show that he is stronger than the instinctual, physical, sexual urge and the emotional needs of that level; a period of fasting, of vegetarianism, of all the various disciplines, to show 'I am master of my body, I am master of my emotions.'

The mind too has to undergo a discipline. It is the discipline in the right use of imagination, because the mind can be a good master but much of the time it makes a pretty lousy master if nothing is disciplining it. It is the old problem of Plato's guardians: who guards the guardians? Who watches the watchers of the race?

The mind can form images that are not at all aligned with reality: worry, anxiety, or pictures of the self which are not consistent with right relations. I can see myself as a dominant leader; and I can harness my emotions, harness my body to this powerful will of my mind, but I can do it in such a way that I become a tyrant. Or I can enter into some mental attitude or vision concerning myself that is not really opening me out to other people, that sees other people as objects to be manipulated, just as it sees its own emotional and physical nature as an object to be manipulated. This, again, can be a necessary stage in the experience of that soul.

The mind, in other words, can form the wrong kind of images and thus harness its energies in what are essentially self-defeating ways on one level, like a person who is continually worrying and all his energies are going into fear; then the fear may reach a point where it begins to dictate the images, and the two bodies reinforce each other in a negative fashion.

One of the functions of the Hierarchy and of all beings who seek to serve the race is to project into the mental consciousness of the race the kind of images that the mind can utilize as tools of self-identification, which at the same time put the mind in closer contact with the soul.

These are images of nobility, Christ-like archetypes, in terms

26

of service, in terms of using the mind to focus on images of divinity, like various thought-forms of masters, of gurus, or maybe just abstract thoughts of truth, justice, like the thought-forms that the Moral Rearmament people use of absolute purity, absolute honesty, absolute love. The mind can form these images and relate to them in such a way that the being is uplifted.

They are still thought-forms and hence ultimately are limiting and will at some point have to be destroyed, but they are thought-forms which cause the mind to organize itself in a progressive fashion and help the mind to discipline the lower energies and organize them in a more constructive way.

When I talk about the need for people to be polarized into the mind, this is really what I am saying. I do not mean that people have to think a lot and read a lot and become brains in an intellectual way, but that they must use their minds to form images that establish for them a centre of identity which is securely and strongly protected so that they can achieve contact with their soul, and they are not simply swayed by the impulses, the energies, the desires, the instincts that move upon mass levels, doing it because it is the thing to do, because the crowd does it. It is the discriminatory evaluative aspect of the mind which gives to the person the freedom to say 'yes' or 'no.'

That freedom can cause pain and suffering. A lot of the pain is caused as the energies of the lower level, the emotional level, the physical level, are being brought into synthesis and harmony and purity. But it saves a lot of suffering later on if this is done.

In point of fact it need not create suffering at all if we know what we are doing and why we are doing it. But many people, using the mind for spiritual purposes, think in terms of self-sacrifice and abstinence and giving up when really what you are trying to do is just what Jesus said: 'Seek ye first the kingdom of God and all else will be added. . . .' Why fritter around with fragmented things which can only satisfy momentary needs when you can go direct to the source that satisfies all needs for all time. The mind can help you to do that if it is used properly. If we think, not in terms of self-sacrifice which is using the mind to identify ourselves as something that has to give up something and therefore as a suffering being, but as creating an image of 'I am moving heroically, joyously into a position of abundance, into a position of greater attunement,' then we have a positive energy and image to work with.

As we in our own lives can demonstrate this, as we project it through our words, as we project it through our actions, these mental images become very strongly re-inforced in the mental life of the race, and the mind then becomes an increasingly more effective bridge and servant. As the person becomes centred within himself, but at the same time knows through his mind that this centring is not a selfish thing, that he is orienting himself outward, then all at once the soul begins to enter.

When I say 'all at once,' it may not happen in a flash. Its entering may take several lives to move. But the soul begins to take increasing command as the mind uses its images, not to enhance itself and say, 'My will, my mental image be done,' but 'I will contact the will of my inner being, my centre.' Then suddenly you begin to find your centre. You begin to find the centre which is really *you*—and yet amazingly enough it is everyone else at the same time.

That is the significant difference between the centre that the mind creates which is a temporary staging base for you to use in your evolution, and your true centre. The mind centre is separative even when it tries not to be; the soul centre is not.

When you feel it, you feel it. There is just no mistaking it. You *know*, even if it is just for a fraction, that you and that other being, or you and that flower, or you and that rock, are part of the same living structure in the universe. There is no denying that knowledge. The mind may reel back from it, and the final struggle

28

begins as the mind which has taken you this far suddenly becomes very reluctant to give up its position as guide and guru and give over to the true master within, the centre within.

You may retreat at times from the full impact of what appears to be a loss of identity, but it is not. It is a loss of the mental image of identity, of what we think we are, the image I have held of myself. This is what David Spangler is.

But the soul could not care less what David Spangler thinks he is. The soul knows what it is—and by God and the soul that is what David Spangler is going to be too, if the soul has anything to say about it!

As this transformation takes place, you may undergo continuing death-like experiences until you just say, 'Right! I surrender. I surrender this energy-need of the mind to form these images. I will now just be open to change, be open to transformation, be open to the whole. I can use my emotions, my mind and my body to augment this. I use my emotions because I can harness my desire towards desiring this wholeness.' Once you have experienced it, even if just for a moment, then you know what it is to desire it and your emotions move with you. They cease to be an obstacle. It is like tasting something that is so delicious that from that point onward, whenever you think of it you feel a desire towards it.

The mind will serve you that way, too, as you form images of yourself, not based on time and space but based on an increasing understanding mentally, emotionally, of your timeless formless reality and invoke this.

With this understanding of these levels of being we have a framework on which we can discuss the flow of energy through these levels which on all levels may be called sex, or the creative energy, or the energy of relationship.

It is important to understand this energy because it is the basic building energy that you have to work with. It will either

29

build for increasing involvement in form, or it will build for you a rhythm of energy that helps you to fulfil your destiny as a transformer of form, that which goes beyond form and yet lifts it and creates the true synthesis between spirit and matter.

Sex and Identity

Man expresses himself on the different levels of the physical and the etheric, the astral or emotional, the mental, and the spiritual. On the level of body and emotion and mind, until a person becomes integrated within himself, he is actually three separate beings because each of the three levels has its own particular pattern of energy, of life, of desire, of identity.

Each level will tend to try and function according to its identity. The physical body will seek out its needs. The emotional body will seek out its rhythm. The mental body will seek out its rhythm. This state of affairs creates within the individual a condition of impurity, of being pulled in a number of directions and not being centred or unified in any one.

Part of the lesson material of spiritual evolution is to learn how to blend together the energies of these different levels so that they function as a wholeness.

The soul, the level above the mind, is in itself pure wholeness. It is the first level on which an individual experiences his true identity, as opposed to his assumed identity. The soul has the ability to synthesize or bring together the different levels of the personality.

This question of identity is a key one for the human race.

31

For humanity is of a dual nature. We are spirit on the one hand, and we are form that has evolved from spirit on the other hand. We are always faced with this question of which is dominant in our nature. This is expressed in different ways in man's culture: does the lower side of man's nature rule? Or is it the higher side?

In this quest for identity the mind comes into play through its capacity to form images. The mind will form images subjectively, and it will then say, 'This is what I am.' This image may be based on experience. For example, I can learn how to speak to people, I can give lectures, and my mind will then say 'I am a lecturer,' or 'I am a teacher,' or 'I am a builder,' or whatever I have been in the past. My mind can identify myself in terms of various definitions: 'I am an American, I am a man, I am a human being.'

The mind will form these images in order to create for itself a sense of being, a sense of identity. Along the route of human evolution this is a very good thing. The mind is the part of us that helps us to go beyond mass consciousness, the instinctive consciousness of the group, and to become at one with the true consciousness of the group which is the soul. The mind, through the exercise of its power of direction, can initiate the rhythms of control and synthesis over the lower nature, the body and the emotions.

There comes a time when the images that the mind forms of itself no longer express the truth about the self or about the individuality. And when an image ceases to encompass for that person at his stage of growth the wholeness of truth with which he can deal, that image becomes an illusion. It may have been an illusion before then to someone else, but it becomes an illusion in fact to an individual when a given mental definition or image ceases to keep pace with his evolutionary needs.

For example, for many people the idea or image of an anthropomorphic God, a father-figure, is a very useful image. It relates them to a divine source which at that point in their

32

evolution they can comprehend. That is a good deal better than not relating to any divine source at all.

To someone else who has gone beyond that, who is thinking in terms of God as a universal Being or universal Spirit, or even as something which cannot be defined at all, the concept of God as a person seems incredibly limiting. One might be justified in saying that it is an illusion.

But it is not an illusion to a person who requires that image at that stage of their development. As they grow and begin to comprehend more about the universe in which they are living, and about themselves and their own divine nature, they have to undergo a process of disillusionment. And disillusionment simply means the shattering of our illusions so that we can begin to see reality, or at least see the next stage of reality for us.*

So the mind serves as the creator of the images which can then harness the energy that comes through the emotional and physical and etheric natures. But at some point all of these images that the mind forms will have to be destroyed if the person is to progress beyond the capacity of those images.

What does this have to do with sex? It has a great deal to do with it because the true challenge of sex is the challenge of identity. Once we get the larger question right of who we are, then all lesser questions as to the right use of energy fall into place.

I want to define for you what I mean by sex and how it manifests on the different levels, how it affects this question of the use of energy on those levels, and the question of identity. We can then go on to discuss the right use of sexual energy and what could be called the ethics or morality of sex.

---

* See *Towards a Planetary Vision.* 'Three of the qualities which the modern disciple must learn are: discipline, or the ability to impose a rhythm or develop a rhythm within one's being; discrimination, or the ability to use the mind to sort out the many energies with which we come in contact; and disillusionment.

What is sex? It is two things. Firstly, it is part of a great universal law. This is the law of attraction which leads to union, which in turn leads to synthesis or oneness, which in turn leads to creation. Secondly, sex is that relationship, that synthesis, which opens the door for life-energy to flow, for vital building-energy to flow into form, whatever form that may be, on whatever level.

How does this work within the structure of an individual's experience? On the physical level we do not exist as a single unified being. Our physical body is a community of beings which has been synthesized by our higher consciousness—the etheric, astral, mental and soul consciousnesses. Therefore the first level on which an individual experiences sex is in that relationship of energy between the various levels of his being that permits them to function to any degree as a wholeness, that allows your mind to work with your emotions, your emotions to work with your body, and so on.

Some force is at work interrelating these essentially different dimensions and vibrations of expression; some force is attracting these bodies together, causing them to enter into some relationship of union, synthesizing them to some degree, and out of that creating your vehicles, your being, your personality.

If it were not for this synthesis of energy, your physical body would manifest what it is in reality—simply a collection of individual units of life, the various cells of your body.

The cells of your body are not, with one exception, bi-sexual. Your cells reproduce themselves through division, through simple fission. One skin cell divides and you have two skin cells. There are those parts of your body which are active enough to provide growth through cellular division. That is something different from what we consider to be sex.

The exception to that is the pattern of cell which carries our hereditary pattern beyond the body—the sperm for the male and the egg for the female. On the physical level it is only these two

34

cellular forms that can experience the fullness of sexual relationship, attraction, union and synthesis which creates. The rest of your cells simply do not have the capacity to destroy themselves in a process of blending with a different cellular form. In other words, you cannot amalgamate with another individual physically and suddenly become one unit—one protoplasmic mass with four arms and four legs.

So on a physical level, speaking now of the manifestation of energy, in one way sex does not exist. What exists is what can be called a 'delivery mechanism' which through the process of evolution has been made highly pleasurable in its physical manifestation so that the race will continue to propagate itself.

As soon as we move beyond the physical level the picture begins to change. The etheric body, the body of vitalization, the body which breathes the energies of life—prana—in and out and vitalizes the cellular tissue and unifies the cellular tissue into a single living community, that body is wholly your own. It is not a collection of units. It is one complete integral energy form.

As such, on the etheric level, the sexual relationship manifests itself as a rhythmical exchange of energy equivalent to breathing. It is this exchange of energy, this vitalization, between individuals during the sexual union that creates what could be called the energy of well-being and of fulfilment on physical levels.

But the same interchange of energy can take place as etheric bodies blend without having to engage in sexual union itself. Many married couples discover this, that often there is a tremendous depth of peace and satisfaction that comes simply from being close to each other. Maybe this is just the exchange of one's nearness, of body warmth. But on the etheric levels an energy exchange is taking place when the consciousnesses through love, through attraction, through union, are open to that exchange. A greater degree of synthesis can occur.

What is created on the etheric levels is not a third etheric

35

body necessarily, but a strengthening, an inflow of energy that strengthens the etheric bodies of the two mates.

On astral levels, emotional levels, we come to the body of feeling which is primarily the body of attraction. It is here that the sexual energy finds a great deal of potency because it is operating in its natural domain, so to speak. The astral body, the desire body, is a body that is designed to respond either towards something or away from something—to put it very simply. Since sex is a manifestation of the law of attraction and of union, we have here an energy that is itself related to the law of attraction.

A good deal of what we call sex and what is spoken of as being 'erotica' is designed to relate to the emotional body and to stimulate desire. In the animal kingdom, for the most part, and certainly in the plant kingdom, the sexual energy is regulated by a pattern of rhythm and timing. On a physical level if the physical body manifests according to its own innate consciousness, it too will tend to function according to rhythm.

But when this is coupled with a highly organized and active emotional desire body as it is in a human being, natural rhythm is replaced by individual rhythm and by the power of emotion moving through a person by desire, and what operates as a sexual energy for a human being becomes now expressed as a desire energy.

The fulfilment of the sexual expression on emotional levels is the satisfaction of a need, satisfaction of the desire impulse. In other words, you have wanted something, you have been motivated to go after it, and you have achieved it.

Actually this does not have to be sex as we understand it at all. It does not have to be physical intercourse. It can be a desire for a good dinner, a desire for a painting, a desire to create a beautiful song. Whatever you can form a relationship of attraction with, and through that create a creative flow of energy and synthesis, you are expressing a sexual relationship with that thing.

On a mental level the mind seeks images. These can be in the form of information and knowledge, or in the form of definition, of actual pictorial concepts—symbolic concepts which we all work with and which express to ourselves certain meanings—as, for example, our self-image. Some may see themselves in different ways: a man may think of himself as a Gregory Peck figure, or a John Wayne figure; a woman may think of herself as Raquel Welch figure or a Twiggy figure.

In other words, you can form an image, a picture based on stimuli supplied by your environment, and this has meaning for you. This may sound funny but it can serve a purpose. If a person, thinking of himself along certain heroic archetypes, can therefore generate the energy to act and accomplish heroically, then that image has served a purpose for him.

But at some point he will have to destroy that image and learn to see himself as he actually is.

On mental levels we can establish direction which helps us to achieve unity in life. Our emotional body is not allowed to simply manifest itself in random attractiveness or repulsion, but we begin to say, 'This is what I will move towards. This is what I will not move towards. This is what I will accept into my life rhythm. This is what I will not accept.'

So the mind can express sexual energy through the building of imagery which controls and directs the total manifestation of energy for the organism, for yourself.

On soul levels the whole picture begins to change. So far we are dealing with levels of consciousness that are fundamentally entrapped in form, and see themselves within the experience of 'This is what I am and that is what you are'—the self and the not-self, 'me and the rest of the world.' Therefore the sexual pattern is expressing as a law of attraction, an attraction between otherwise divided elements. As such the sexual expression is a manifestation of the law of love, the energy of love. The law of attraction is a manifestation of the law of love.

But on the soul level the picture changes because the soul does not perceive itself as being separate from its world. That is the definition of the soul and of its higher levels of the spiritual being: that it is not experiencing the distinction between the self and the not-self. What it is experiencing is simply the self and all things are the self.

The personality levels—body, etheric, emotion, mind—create relationships from the outside in: the soul creates relationships from the inside out. The soul of each of us is one with each other and so the synthesis is already achieved. What may yet have to be achieved is how to work with this synthesis in order to create.

So there are soul marriages that are formed, soul links, in which a particular kind of energy is related between the souls involved in order to create a form. For example, Findhorn is very much the product of a group of souls coming together to work through the personality structure to create a community. We are so diverse in our personalities and in our backgrounds and in our beliefs that if we had to depend upon the law of attraction, on personality levels, many of us would not be here, or having arrived would not stay!

But from the level of the soul comes this intrinsic and basic knowledge that we are one, and that knowledge helps us to over-ride and work creatively with the differences that we have between us.

In the quest for identity the mind will use the energy that it has to form images of itself. And the second aspect of sex is that it opens the door for vitalization and building. A fundamental sexual relationship that each of us undergoes is that between the mind and the emotions.

If you form an image and it does not stir you emotionally in such a way that you can identify with it emotionally, then you are not going to keep that image. If I tell you that you are such-and-such and you do not believe me, you may accept it intellectually

38

but it does not stir anything on emotional levels. No energy has been released and that image does not really mean anything to you.

If I say that you are a divine being, and you can accept that with your mind but emotionally you realize that you are not, that image is worthless until such time as you can realize with your feeling nature that 'yes, I really am a divine being, I really am one with God.' This vitalizes the image. A relationship is set up within your own psychological structure and through that relationship energy is released.

This energy may change your life. It may give you new direction. It may uplift you. Or it can work negatively. You may adopt images and emotionally react to images which are depressive, which are limiting, which make you feel antagonistic towards yourself. This too releases an energy but an energy of negative building.

What I wish to communicate is that once this link and flow of energy is created between mind and feeling, a vital energy is released which builds. It creates the structure of that image. It vitalizes it. It gives it strength. As a consequence that image will begin to act upon you with that strength. This is one of the reasons why it is so hard to change your mind about certain things, to overcome conditioning, to overcome habit patterns: that having created them in the first place and vitalized them, you are in essence combating yourself. You are attempting to use energy to destroy something that you are creating at the same time.

Through this internal sexual relationship, vital energy is released and it goes towards building our sense of identity.

When we come in the next chapter to some of the laws which underlie the basic ethics of sexual expression, we shall find that they are laws related to this concept that through the utilization of all our energies we build our sense of identity. We either build it in such a way that we are freed by that identity, that it is a stepping stone which helps us to grow, or we build it in such a way that it becomes a prison house. The wrong use of sexual energy, whether it is in relationships within a person or relationships with other people, is a wrong use because we are utilizing the energy of relationship and of creative building to substantiate our identification with form.

The early mystics in Christianity and other religions too focused in on this. Out of this came a certain realization that the sexual expression tends to keep man on a physical level, and therefore if a person wishes to become spiritual he has to learn to control and discipline the body. Out of this has developed the whole tradition of celibacy.

This is both true and untrue. It is true if we are identifying ourselves sexually in such a way that we remain tied to our form nature, our desires, our body, our mentality. It is not true if we can use the energies that we have of life, of attraction, of synthesis, of oneness, to make us aware of increasing oneness, of greater wholeness, and to link us with the soul.

One of the identities that each of us works within is the identity of oneself as a sexual being. We are either male or female, and that tends to be the limit to which we carry our concept of sex. If there is one concept which I would wish to communicate to you, it is that your sexual nature embraces almost everything that you are. You are a being who is in a state of constant relationship with your universe—a relationship on all levels of embracing, of attraction, of repulsion—and out of that relationship you are creating your future, your experience pattern, your wisdom, your knowledge.

Many of the problems that arise in the context of sexual energy and desire arise because we can see sexual fulfilment only in physical terms. This is inevitable if we are identifying sex purely as a physical energy and a physical action. If we are identifying sex in that way, we are not using that energy rightly. We are using it to keep our consciousness tied to a physical form.

When you consider that the soul is a manifestation of group consciousness, of universal love and wisdom, what happens when you touch the energy of your soul and begin to invoke it through the personality? How is your personality going to withstand the descent of a love that sees everyone and everything you meet as part of you, and as it stimulates the personality simply augments the whole rhythm of attraction?

It can create true challenges for the personality. How does one resolve these challenges? You cannot go to bed with everyone! Do you simply move with the emotional pattern as it directs under the stimulation of your soul's approach? If that is so, the soul will not approach. You cannot attune yourself to your higher nature until such time as your personality is secure enough that the energy of the higher nature will not disrupt you.

It is the same principle that was expressed in the Bible, that you could not enter the innermost precincts of the temple and come face to face with God, for you would be destroyed. Only the priests could do that and then only once a year, as they were presumably purified for this and were capable of withstanding this energy.

This is symbolic of the relationship between you and your soul. How can you as a personality deal with the energy of love which you are trying to attune to, the energy of the higher nature? You can only deal with it if your understanding of the laws of attraction and love are expanded to where you see all aspects of your being and all kinds of function and relationship as capable of transmitting energy, of establishing a circulation of energy.

A sexual relationship can be a touch, it can be a look, it can be a shared thought, it can be joining together to create, like a community, or to create within a project.

It is the mind that is going to determine this. If the mind is thinking of itself, has formed an image of itself, of this individuality and its love expression, its sexual expression, within the limited terms: bounded on the one side by the physical organs, and on the other side by one's emotional capacity and desire nature, then your identity is not sufficient to cope with your true spiritual identity. Yet one of the healthiest experiences an individual can undergo is to realize that he or she can love many people and love them simultaneously and equally though uniquely in each case.

How can one handle an experience like that without creating social disruption and chaos within the body of the social whole? The personality cannot handle it unless it is using this energy and interpreting it not as meaning a flow out to someone, but a revelation of one's own inner nature, one's own identity.

If I feel a love flow with you, I can interpret it in two ways: it can mean 'I love you. I, subject, flow to you, object, across a gap'; or it can mean 'I *am* love.' This energy which we are recognizing is a revelation of the fact that I *am* love and that is my identity. And I am wisdom, and I am light. As a person learns to answer the basic question, 'Who am I after all?' the problem of sex begins to dissolve and disappear. If you know who you are, that you are a soul being, you can draw into yourself the needs and desires of the lower levels instead of allowing them simply to project outward. You can see that instead of relating to the world as a set of objects, you can relate to the world as if it is part of you—which in fact it is.

Each of the levels has its own needs, or set of needs, according to the energy which it represents. The physical body needs food, needs nourishment. All the levels need nourishment of some kind. But relationship that is built on need is not a good relationship, if by that we mean a relationship that is built on the wrong use of one's mental power of identity.

Most of what we consider to be our needs are only what we think are our needs and are contained within our definition of ourself, often based on past experience. Let us say: I had a bad childhood, I was not loved. Therefore my identity of myself is that I need love. Some level, some part of me, is saying that I need love, and I will gravitate towards someone who seems to give me that love.

But the problem with this is that once I have identified this as being 'me,' identity is the most important possession we have on the personality level and we will fight to hold it. If we were not so afraid of being destroyed, we would be making faster union with our higher nature.

But we fight for our personal will, for our personal identity. If the need that I understand myself as having is part of that identity: for years I have thought of myself as the one who needs love, or the one who needs this, or the one who needs something else—then no relationship in the world is going to satisfy that. Even if someone is giving me love, I will always want more. Even if someone is giving me sex, I will want more. Even if someone is giving me food, or money, or warmth, or information—once I have identified need as part of me, once it has been incorporated into my identity structure, it is insatiable. I cannot be satisfied.

This is what I mean when I say that a relationship based on need alone is not good.

On the other hand all relationships are based on true need. We are each part of a whole and our true need is to find the other parts of that whole so that we can function in wholeness.

That wholeness may be two people, ten people, a hundred people, a race, three million people. Whatever it may be, we each do have valid needs. But many of our needs are unconscious. We are not aware of them or we do not think about them much. And when we come into contact with someone who can really fulfil those needs, even ones we do not know we have, we experience a tremendous sense of rightness about the relationship—a blending, an instinctive drawing together, like two pieces of a jigsaw puzzle that fit on one level or another.

So we are satisfying each other's needs. The point is not to identify ourselves as being in need, as needful beings. For then we have identified ourselves with lack.

When this happens the sexual energy is one of the basic energies that we will try to use, on one level or another, to satisfy this sense of lack. In so doing we are using sex to maintain an identity of need rather than to build and reveal an identity of wholeness.

Within our divine nature we are whole. Once I have a sense of my abundancy, that I am whole, I am at peace, for I know that everything I have need of comes. A basic principle for understanding and dealing with the question of identity and sex as it relates to it is expressed in something Jesus said: 'Seek ye first the kingdom of heaven and all else is added.' That is a fundamental statement of the basic law of manifestation. Seek after truth, the realization of who you are, your identity, and everything that you think you have need of or really have need of comes to you.

That truth will dispel any illusions you have about yourself: wrong images of identity; and it will reveal the true pattern of who you are and the relationships that you must create in your world if you are to fulfil the reason that you have come to birth.

The Morality of Love

Jesus is remembered for many things: his life, his death, his resurrection, the teachings he gave, the example which he provided. One of the things he said, when asked which of the commandments was the greatest, was that there was only one commandment that man should follow and that was: to love God with all one's heart and strength, and to love one's neighbour as oneself. He said that if that one commandment was obeyed man would fulfil all the others.

Through the centuries since he lived many systems of philosophy and ethics and morality have developed, but in this simple statement which Jesus gave and which is echoed by other great prophets in other religious systems lies the heart of what it is all about. If you were to remove from the human heritage that one statement and the thought which it represents, and attempted to replace it with ethical and moral and philosophical systems which did not express that statement, man would be left with nothing.

In discussing the concepts of sex and human relationships and morality, this statement—to love God with all one's heart and strength and to love one's neighbour as oneself—is a foundational statement.

Why is this so? One reason is that within that rather vast

45

conceptual structure to which this statement is the key lies an understanding of man's true identity. The function of all religious and philosophical and ethical systems that have been divinely promoted has been to reveal to man his identity.

In the beginning, to speak in allegorical fashion, there existed the One. That One was unknowable, without form, without substance—as we would understand form and substance.

From this One proceeded two, and duality was created. Out of this basic consciousness of polarity, or manifestation of polarity, relationship evolved: positive and negative, male and female, spirit and matter.

These dualities, these two extremes and all of the different levels of interrelationship between, established a generating source from which creation could spring. That generating source is the relationship between these two.

One of the basic religious symbols, ancient in its origin, in fact non-human in its origin, is the symbol of the trinity: father, mother, son—the duality out of which springs the creative substance from which universes may be built. The interrelationship between spirit and matter, between the polarities, creates a phenomenon which we call consciousness; and out of consciousness can be built the bridge that leads man from one level of identity to another.

Sex, as defined in the last chapter, is a manifestation of the law of attraction, and it represents a particular kind of relationship. It represents a relationship within consciousness that goes through attraction, union, synthesis and then creativity, the release of the product, or the result of the synthesis and the union.

Sex exists only because the polarities exist and the awareness of polarity, the awareness of duality. There must be that which is attracting and that which is being attracted. There must be two things which in some fashion are separate in order for them to come together and be unified and achieve a synthesis. Therefore

46

there is a similarity between sex, which is a manifestation of the laws governing the synthesis of opposites, and consciousness which is also born of the synthesis of the opposites of duality.

It is said in occult tradition that the sexual energy, on whatever level it is functioning, is the most fundamentally powerful of all the energies with which humanity can deal. The reason for this is that it is linked with the substance of consciousness. It is not untrue to say that your consciousness, your awareness, your sense of being, is the product of sexual manifestation. It is the product of spirit and matter coming together and interrelating in such a way that the third force is released—and that third force is life and consciousness. The two are interchangeable in occult terms.

Sex is a building force and when we discuss the right use of sexual energy we discuss it in terms of this concept of building. Whether an energy is used rightly or not is entirely dependent on what is created from it, and how that creation reverberates on the creator and on the creator's environment.

For man is on a pilgrimage in consciousness to learn what it means to be a creator, to become completely master of the sexual energy on whatever level that energy manifests, to be a master of relationships and a master of all the laws that govern relationship— and there are many. What we call sex on the physical level is simply a small facet of one of these laws.

There are certain things which a creator must know. He must know what it is that he is creating, how he is creating it, how it affects himself and how it affects his world. He must understand the laws of wisdom, of balance, of love.

Man's history, and the religious ethical systems which have guided him upon his history, may be seen as revelation from higher consciousness intended to shepherd man in this steady unfolding of his understanding of himself as a creator, as a god. Jesus said this quite clearly when he said, 'ye are gods.'

When man was functioning in a way that was fundamentally

47

emotional, fundamentally through his astral body, man was then polarized, or functioning within a state of consciousness that found its identity in terms of its environment. All the lower levels of consciousness find identity in terms of objective reality: things that can be perceived, things that can be felt, whether emotionally or physically, images which the mind can create.

These lower bodies, the personality vehicles, incorporate into themselves from experience the material which is then used to fabricate identity. We take in memories and say 'I am this person who had these experiences. This is what I am.' If you have amnesia and forget all you have experienced, you still know that you exist but you have a sense of 'Who am I?' You have no past.

It is the soul and its higher levels which represent the levels that do not look to the environment for the substance of identity. The soul does not say 'I am that' and then look around to see just what that may be. The soul says 'I am what I am, the source of identity.'

For that reason the soul is non-acquisitive. It has no need to acquire anything because it is all things. The laws of abundance and manifestation proceed from the realization within a person's consciousness that he is one with his soul which is limitless abundance.

When man was very young as an evolving being his identity was supplied for him within certain structures: social structures, religious structures, ethical structures. Man was governed from outside his consciousness because he had not yet learned how to contact his own higher nature and discover his identity and be self-governing.

As a consequence the early divine revelations all emphasized law and morality based on law. Whole cultures would be governed by very minute and detailed descriptions of how a person should or should not act, until almost every moment of the day and every conceivable action that a person could enter into in his culture was

48

covered by some form of regulation.

A good deal of our morality now is the heritage from those early days, but in our present world there is a definite reaction against traditional forms of law and ethics and morality.

This kind of reaction has probably always existed in each new generation as it comes along, as it seeks to establish its own identity within the scheme of Earth's history. But in our time this quest is particularly intensified because the whole meaning of the New Age is that man makes a transition in consciousness from relying upon external authority to being centred and relying upon internal attunement with his world and with his soul, with his divine nature.

Much challenge that arises within the field of morality and ethics where individuals are concerned comes from the fact that there is a certain natural knowing within the human being, within some people more than others, that at some point each of us has to learn to stand on his own spiritual two feet and be himself a revealer of the divine presence, of the God within, and the balance, the wisdom, the love, the whole pattern of attunement to one's world which that divine represents.

As this sense of eventual independence on one level stirs within an individual, whether it is unconscious or conscious, there is a reaction against structures of externally imposed law. Most laws, certainly ethical laws, were set forth for the race to provide a definite structure within which individuals could learn to discipline and control their lower vehicles and give the soul a chance to get its energy down and anchored—at which point the person gains his own control.

I will give a physical analogy of this. People who have been stricken with an illness that has made them weak, having been in bed for a long time, may find upon arising that they no longer have the strength in their legs to support them. So the doctor will give them leg-braces and various exercises to strengthen the muscles. The leg braces are designed to support the individual until he can stand. They are augmentations of his own inner strength and they are designed in the analogy that I am using to be eventually removed. They are meant only to help a person to gain his own strength. The doctor must be wise in knowing when to remove them so that they do not create further weakness.

The laws that govern the race are the same. They are braces within which a person can find an energy of direction, of discipline, of standard of action, which he may not yet be able to supply for himself through his own intrinsic wisdom and awareness. Remove that from an individual and quite often you end up with a person who becomes psychologically weak. When the lower vehicles are allowed simply to act as they wish, you end up with a person who has no identity at all in a real sense. He is responding or reacting to influences from the environment, reacting to pleasure, to pain, to likes, to dislikes without any real sense of what is happening.

At some point the braces must be removed. The New Age represents for many people a collective removal of certain of the braces, for it is considered that now individuals are strong and mature and able to stand in the strength of their attunement.

It is the role of a centre like Findhorn and other centres of this nature to be a place where people can come and experience certain disciplines of attunement and group awareness, so that they can go out into the world again strengthened and able to stand on their own spiritual feet.

The challenge which is faced may be described thus: man is a receptacle of energy which is continually pouring into him from one level or another as his various bodies take in nourishment, take in awareness of the environment on many levels. This energy has to do something. It has to go somewhere. It has to be utilized.

The challenge is for the person to utilize the energies of his life, of his consciousness, in such a way that his divine identity is revealed and his personality identity becomes illumined within that revelation and ceases to be a disunified element operating on its own.

Within this context where does morality as it concerns sex enter a discussion of the New Age?

The lawgivers have always been upon this planet and many laws have been given to us. There comes a time when men must learn to resolve all the laws into one as Jesus did, into one pillar of internal attunement and strength which can support his flight as a soul and make him a winged being. To me that is what it is all about.

It is not a question of 'Should there be sex between two people in marriage, outside marriage, with more than two people?' Morality, when viewed not as a structure of law but in terms of what morality is intended to achieve in the destiny of the race, is simply an expression of 'What does it take to help a human being realize his greater and winged identity? How can a human being break free of the prisons of form consciousness and limited consciousness and begin to function as a true son of God?'

What does sex do? On each level in which it expresses it creates a relationship. It establishes a bond. It sets up a rhythm. It is a building energy. It is a vitalizing energy. It is the same thing as throwing open a door and receiving an energy like sunlight which, when it strikes upon a living seed, causes it to grow.

It is a creative force. It is not creative in itself. It is the energy that permits creative manifestation to take place. Sex does not create. It simply opens the pathways through which vitalization can be made to manifest, through which a divine reality can be made manifest. Whatever exists or is functioning within an individual when such vitalizing energy is received by the consciousness it becomes nourished.

This is the same thing as saying that if you expose a garden to sunlight and to rain and to the nourishment of the soil, whatever seeds are in that garden are going to grow. It is important for man

51

now, if he is to free himself, to realize that he must confront tne challenge of his sexual identity and deal with it and expand that identity.

The problem is not one of sexual relationships. It is one of 'How do I perceive myself as a sexual being who is having these relationships? Do I perceive myself within a pattern of need? Do I perceive myself within a pattern of physical instinct? Do I perceive myself as functioning within a pattern of a particular sexual framework—by which I mean that sex is simply a physical intercourse and other forms of relationships are something else again? Am I seeing myself only in terms of my emotional mental nature and therefore relating to my world in that way?'

A wrong sexual relationship is any relationship which is built on wrong identity, wrong identification. This would be motives which are not open to creating balance, wholeness, oneness. It is a consciousness that sees other people as objects which can satisfy needs or lacks within oneself, a consciousness that sees life and the various manifestations of life as a great grab-bag from which one reaches in and extracts what is necessary, without thought as to the condition of that reservoir.

It is the same kind of consciousness that pursues material production at the expense of the ecological environment. It boils down to a selfish, self-oriented consciousness—which does not have to be necessarily a person who is grasping, who is nasty, who hits small children and kicks dogs! It can be a person who is simply not conceiving of himself as anything other than a separate unit apart from the world in which he lives and from which he derives his nourishment. He is not seeing that he is in some fashion an integral part of that world, contributing to it and in fact having to contribute to it if he is to survive and to grow and to become more than what he is at the moment—working out of a fantasy consciousness rather than out of a clear conception of the needs and the reality of one's environment and of other people in the environment. For when any kind of vitalizing building energy flows through that kind of consciousness, it reinforces it.

Sex and love, emotional relationships and mental relationships between people, can be used to create wholeness. If this were not so we would be in a very bad shape as an evolving race. But it is so. People can come together motivated purely by personality attachment, and through the experiences that are gained together and the wisdom that is gained begin to unfold to greater levels of consciousness. Love interpreted in a personality way and sex desire—all these various manifestations can be used to move towards and create a sense of wholeness.

But the identity that we are seeking to realize is that we are already whole, and therefore the relationships that we create can be seen as expressions of that wholeness, not as mechanisms to try and build it or create it.

Earlier I said that one of the things that a god has to know is what it is he is creating and how he is creating it and how it is affecting his environment. In essence a god has to have a consciousness of wholeness. He has to see himself not as a separate entity from that which he is creating, but as a part of it, as one with it, and responsible for it because he is one with it.

The lesson that we are each trying to learn and are learning is how to develop and expand our consciousness of the whole, awareness of the whole, whatever wholeness that may be of which we are a part. It may be a family unit, a wife, a husband, children, parents; it may be a community unit, a national unit, the universe —however much your consciousness can encompass in terms of 'this is the whole of which I am a part.'

The lesson that your consciousness is here to learn is, 'How can I contribute to and be at one with this wholeness?' Relationship on this level, on most levels, is the way in which we do contribute to and manifest this wholeness.

Our relationships themselves must be clear and able to

demonstrate that we are creating this relationship with an awareness of the reality that is already behind it.

An experience that many people have as they move in spiritual studies is to encounter someone and within a matter of minutes, perhaps within a matter of seconds, they know that they have a relationship with that person which in depth and intensity is equivalent to the kind of relationship which on ordinary personality levels is usually created only after years of acquaintance. You just know in that instant that you are one with that individual. There is a bond, a link. You have done nothing apparently in the moment to create that bond, but in coming together you have revealed it. You have opened a doorway through which reality could be made manifest. In that moment of revelation you are touching that flow of energy, that substance, that illumination which is the presence of the whole, the presence of the Divine.

It may immediately become understood and interpreted and dealt with through your personality consciousness in whatever way that is oriented; but for a moment you experienced what it is like to know timeless and causeless union—union that is there because you are living beings and part of the whole, not because of anything that has taken place in time or any cause that you have initiated.

In pursuing our personality relationships with a consciousness that sees ourselves only as personalities, and using the sexual energy whether it is on a physical level or an emotional level or a mental level to create relationships and to follow through on our personality directions, we are running the risk of denying ourselves these peak experiences.

How open are we to loving one another? Not desiring one another, not chasing after one another, not forming mental images of one another which are appealing, but how open are we to actually loving one another, in stillness affirming the fact that we are one and acting on that basis?

54

Because that is the heart of morality. That is true selflessness. That is true opening up and giving of the self not in sacrifice but in realization of the fact that we are one self. We are *the* self.

As we move into the new age, the structures of law that have been part of our history and heritage will continue because many people still require them. They are still at a point where they are not strong enough to stand without the use of some kind of bracing and assisting structure. But increasingly the race will shed its crutches as those who do catch the vision throw away theirs and begin to live as beings seeking attunement.

Now attunement does not only mean going up and down between me and God. Attunement is created through the ability to create in our human level relationships the qualities that we want to attune to on higher levels. If I want to attune to wisdom, to love, to divine intelligence, I must learn how to use wisdom and love and intelligence in my human relationships. I must set up a pattern, a template, a matrix on this level which can attract its complementary part from a higher level.

Attunement is awareness. Here our sexuality is our greatest assistant, our greatest tool for awareness. If we are using our sexual nature in terms of seeking a mate or seeking pleasure or seeking simply a relationship which is nice and comfortable and warm in the moment, then we may be and probably are using this tool in such a way that we are diminishing our awareness, not increasing it. The reason for this is that your mind and your desire structure, your emotional body, are rather focused instruments. You cannot desire more than a few things at a time, and you cannot actually hold in consciousness the image of more than one thing at a time—even though that 'at a time' may be very brief, a matter of seconds.

Unless the mind is trained, unless the being is opened out on other levels, you are really rather a one-pointed individual, rather narrow focused. How much can you hold in your consciousness at any one moment? How much are you aware of? How much have you forgotten?

You see something in a store. It appeals to you. You think 'Oh I really like that. In fact I like it better than anything else I have seen today.' Then you go to visit another store and you see something that is even more glamorous, even more beautiful and you say 'That is what I like. That is the best thing I have seen today.' What happened to the first thing? It is out of consciousness. It has been replaced. It is this kind of manifestation, of characteristic, which keeps an individual's vision on the level of form, and only a few forms at a time, instead of into the level of the whole.

The consciousness of wholeness and attunement does not mean thinking of other people all the time or thinking of the group all the time. It does not mean that 'if I am to be aware of the whole I must sacrifice my self-awareness.' What it means is that you live with an increasingly expanded awareness of what your world constitutes and what is happening in that world and how you are a part of it: that the life in the flowers and in the trees, the life in the building and the life in the people that surround you is your life, part of your being, and you can love them as you would yourself.

Since you are both part of the Divine Being, when you love God with all your strength you are really lifting your consciousness in such a way that you are learning to love your true identity with sufficient strength to propel you into that identity.

Each individual will find his way to himself according to the dictates of his heart and mind. He will use the aid of external authority when needed. He will rely on himself when he thinks that is best. He will make mistakes at times; he will become blind and move in ignorance; at other times he will become illuminated and move in wisdom.

The function of morality is not to create a system of

judgement, it is to create a system of helpful and identity-promoting discrimination. It is not to enable us all to have a handy check list so that we can determine how our nextdoor neighbour is behaving and whether he is living up to what God expects of him; it is designed to help us to determine whether we are living up to the fullness of what we are.

Jesus said something else that was very interesting. It was after the resurrection when the fishermen were out fishing and they saw him on the shore of the Sea of Galilee. They rowed to shore and of course they were very happy to see him. During the conversation that took place Jesus told them to go and feed his sheep. Peter made a remark about, 'What of these other people, what are they supposed to be doing?' Jesus said, 'Never mind about them. You do what you are supposed to be doing and let the others take care of themselves. I will watch over them; you watch over yourself.'

Morality is often interpreted by people as what others should be doing. As a consequence it never works very well in human society. But love is an awareness of 'How am I functioning as a contributing part of the whole? Is what I am doing and saying and manifesting lifting the consciousness of the group of which I am a part?' We do not have to become sombre about it; the person who is too sombre and serious about being religiously holy is likely to be a dead weight.

We grow through joy and through realization of the bliss of life. By the same token we grow through our awareness.

Sex on all levels—attraction emotionally or mentally; mental images that are formed and then we fall in love with them and they become our identity, our prize package of ideas that we are very reluctant to let go when we have outgrown them; physical intercourse—all of these patterns of energy represent one of the most powerful energies that man has to deal with in the three lower worlds. For it is the basic energy of relationship.

57

Consciousness is born out of relationship. Man is consciousness ascending, therefore he seeks relationship. At the heart of his personality consciousness is the energy of sex.

I do not mean this in a Freudian sense. I am using sex in the esoteric sense as referring to the laws that govern relationship and what is created from relationship and the attractions that bring relationships about. We can control these. We can create these. Depending on the relationships we form and their quality and character is the energy that we release into ourselves and into our environment that determines what we become and whether we build towards our higher nature or whether we continue to build the forms that get us about down here but never get us anywhere.

Love, as Jesus pointed out, is truly the only morality. Love is awareness of the whole, action that takes place in terms of the whole. You are part of the whole, therefore love of the whole is the same as love of self but now approached from a different point of view. It is the self that has learned that if it is to spread its wings all the lives that surround it make up its feathers. It can only go as high as these lives are united to that individual through his or her centre of love and wisdom and awareness.

The next chapter will develop this point further in the context of marriage.

Within each of us, born out of many years and lifetimes of experience, is a centre of wisdom, of awareness and of love—a treasure house filled with things that we can give to our world.

When we give these things we are uplifted. We become more and more the divinity that we are in reality.

We can give much on the level of form, much through our personality, born of the personality. We can give ideas. We can give emotions. We can give physical contact and physical objects. But all these things are transient. They move us along the way but they are not important in themselves. Our tendency is to identify with them and to use our creative power to enhance and maintain that

58

identification.

Divine morality based on a greater awareness of love was given to man to help him to break free of that kind of identification. Sex is only a challenge where man is identifying himself with the wrong things in his life and is seeking to maintain that identity.

As man becomes, in his awareness and recognition and in his action, the soul which he is in reality, all forms of energy-challenges of relationships begin to fall into place and to assume their right proportion and their right use.

The soul is a group consciousness. It is oriented towards the whole. Group consciousness is not created by a group of people coming together. It is created by an unfoldment from within the soul—a true group consciousness which in turn causes the physical units of that group to come together. It is a matter of which comes first, the chicken or the egg. You cannot create the wholeness; you can only reveal it because the wholeness is your true state and identity.

The soul, being a group consciousness, manifests the energies of good will, of wisdom and balance—by which I mean the use of energy in such a way that each person is fulfilled and blessed within their functional part of the whole. No one gains at the expense of others. It is a synergetic situation, in which synthesis and blending takes place for the fulfilment of each.

The soul generates an energy of that kind of motive which establishes a relationship in order that the wholeness may be revealed. This may satisfy the needs that we have; it may satisfy needs we are not even aware that we have; but it will not create for us a consciousness of need. It will not create for us a consciousness that this relationship is important simply because it satisfies certain needs, but it is important because it is a gateway through which the whole is made manifest.

As you each continue in your life pattern to be aware of the unfoldment of your greater self and of the unfoldment of the

59

collective greater self of man which we are now calling the New Age, you will find unfolding equally in your consciousness that rhythm of self-government, of self-awareness and of attunement which will make you a truly moral being—not in terms of law or in terms of ethic but in terms of the God-life that lives within you and lives within me and makes us one.

Creativity and Marriage

Let us take a rose as the starting point for our thoughts. A rose comes to us as the complement of a divine thought and a divine process. This is the process that we call creativity.

Undoubtedly a great deal of imagination and energy and life and work go into creating a rose, into creating all the roses that bless our world and all the other plants as well.

All of these plants come to us via a seed—a seed that contains within itself physically and spiritually that idea which, when translated into form, becomes a rose. Some kind of work is done to enable that idea to take this form.

All creativity proceeds from a seed state through a rhythm of energy, a rhythm of work, that can best be called concentration. A rose, in other words, has to conceive of itself and harness its energies towards being a rose. A rose by any other name might smell as sweet, but a rose that thought of itself by any other picture would not end up as a rose.

I realize that I am anthropomorphizing a bit! But there is a consciousness behind the rose which has conceived the form that it is taking and in the silence of its indwelling being it holds that thought and it holds no other thought. All of its energies flow to the perfection of what it is proclaiming itself to be.

61

A secret of creativity, then, is to be able to harness energies in such a way that they flow to a point and see an idea through to its completion. If metaphorically speaking halfway in its growth the rose suddenly decided that it wanted to be a dandelion, or decided that it wished to exist in some other part of the garden, it would not end up a very good rose. It would not end up a very good dandelion either!

Man can learn a lot from observing the rhythm and harmony and the application of energy that is manifested in nature, because man is an embodiment of the creative principle. Each of us, like the rose but to a far greater degree, represent God in flesh and we possess the ability to form our own images. By giving to them our life energy, our interest, our intent, our love, we can cause these images to take life and form in our world.

One of our functions on Earth is to learn how to utilize this ability to the glory of the divinity which we truly are, how to reveal our true identity as sons of God and not only sons and daughters of nature. Man is given many ways through which he can learn how to exercise his creative powers; how to harness and utilize, in such a way that it reveals his divine identity, the powers of image forming, of utilizing duality to create union and synthesis and thereby to open the portals through which vitalizing life can pour; how to express himself as a god using the basic creative forces of a god.

One of these creative forces is the force of sex. And one of the experiences in which man can best learn how to express his godliness is the experience of marriage.

What is marriage?

For many people in western society marriage is an institution which appears to be on its way out. In some places statistics show that one out of every four marriages end in divorce. There is a growing sentiment amongst people that perhaps this institution of union and the affirmation of union between a man and a woman is no longer practicable in our modern civilization.

But before we consider that question and whether or not marriage is something that can be extended into the new age, let us go back to our first question and come to a definition of what marriage is, why it came into being in the first place, and what it represents in man's long journey of self-learning to reveal his creative power.

In different cultures marriage takes different forms and fulfils different ritualistic parts of the culture. Esoterically when we investigate this concept of marriage, not through studying the history books of man's past but through the insights of a higher consciousness, we must go back to a time in the history of human evolution when a creative decision was made to accelerate the development of the race.

The first and primary marriage which a person experiences is the marriage of his own being, his own identity. Man in his unillumined state, his unintegrated state, is really four beings in one. He is the original group marriage: a physical entity, an emotional entity, a mental entity or level of energy and interest and direction, and the soul, the centre point, the source of ultimate synthesis and wholeness.

Each of these levels, and the vehicles or bodies that are created upon them, and the elemental intelligences that represent these vehicles, must find a way of working together. They must be attracted together. They must unify. They must undergo some form of synthesis, harmonious interworking, before there can take place the manifestation of a human being, or of any other living being that has anything other than just a physical body.

Man is an exercise in the integration of different rates of vibration and energy, all of which come together to form a multi-levelled expression for the use of the soul.

It is not particularly easy to integrate these levels. A long period of evolution is taken in achieving it, and not just human

63

evolution. But there does come a time when it is at last achieved and the human being steps forth upon the stage of human history. Even then that human being has to learn so to blend these energies that he reaches a point where they are not four distinct levels all functioning with relative degrees of harmony but one manifestation reflecting the essential oneness of man's divine nature.

The expression that enables man to achieve this oneness is a form of sexual expression between the levels of his own being. It is the law of attraction at work that draws to each individual the energy that responds to the vibrations that he sets up through his thoughts and feelings, and through that attraction incorporates that energy into him in such a way that his bodies are nourished and built. Through the attraction of the different levels bodies are enabled to work together: mind can work with emotion, emotion can work with the etheric and physical body, and all of these can work with the soul. Increasingly synthesis takes place.

When the final and ultimate point of synthesis is achieved, man has absolute union. What is created is no longer a human being but what must be called a super-human being—an individual who is pure soul functioning through a physical form. That is the definition of a master.

Each of us within ourselves is involved in a marriage process. Each of us combines within ourselves positive and negative, or male and female, elements working together to create the point of final synthesis and oneness.

There came a time when this pattern became objectified into man's environment. Esoterically we say that the division of the sexes took place. Upon the physical plane differentiation of form into a bi-polar expression occurred. This was a very long time ago and it actually occurred before man had a physical body in the way that we now have physical bodies.

From that point man could learn how to utilize the law of attraction, of union, of synthesis—which he had to learn in order to apply it within himself for his own inner illumination and unfoldment—by experiencing it outwardly, experiencing it in his environment, by actually making it part of his very necessary and important human constitution. God created man and he created woman and the two were destined to come together to form the external mating which is the symbol of the internal marriage through which the soul and the personality become one.

The challenge of the individual is to learn how to integrate his body, his emotions, his mind and his spirit—in other words how to achieve purity, how to achieve wholeness. This is not an easy task and it requires many lifetimes for its fruition, for its accomplishment: how to love, how to wield love, how to use wisdom, how to wield will and purpose and intent, not only in the environment but within oneself, and how to use it rightly.

Attunement is a process not only of reaching upward to attune to something that is subjective and spiritual, but reaching outward to experience and relationship with external things, people, events. For man to be whole he must learn how to love himself in balance and wisdom. He must learn how to exercise will and intelligence throughout his nature. But he can best learn this by learning how to express love with balance and wisdom, how to express will and intelligence to others.

It is either a vicious circle or a blessed one depending on how you look at it. If you do not love yourself, you cannot love other people very well; and if you do not love other people very well, you cannot love yourself. On the other hand if you can love other people and act with wisdom, with care, with intelligence towards them, then you can do the same towards yourself and vice versa.

Man has his inner problem objectified and it takes the form of relationships. This challenge of uniting these various energy bodies is challenging enough, just for a person acting within himself, but when it comes to relating to another person the problem is doubled. My mental body not only has to learn how to integrate with my emotions and my physical form and my soul, it has to learn how to integrate with someone else's mental body, someone else's emotion, someone else's body, someone else's soul.

This is true for each of the levels. It becomes a problem in communication. It becomes a challenge in communion. How can I blend what I am with what someone else is? Two forms coming together so that through that blending, through the re-creation of the basic divine archetype of the two poles coming together, father-mother coming together to create the son, we can release the creative force that blesses both of us and creates a third energy —this third energy being the energy of illumination.*

Knowing that this was a challenge the early guardians of the race instituted the concept of marriage. The concept of marriage means simply union between two people blessed and sanctified by God, by a spiritual force. The initiator or priest, whoever had the power to wield the energies of higher levels, performed a ceremony, a ritual, an invocation of blessing for the couple which had the effect of opening certain centres within the bodies and unifying the energies of these bodies so that the couple had that basic blessing, that basic energy of unity, to work with.

It was like a person taking two radio stations, two radio receiving sets, and fine-tuning them so that they could receive together, and then sending them on their way. That was one of the basic purposes behind the institution of marriage.

The second dealt with the propagation of the race. The races of man are of a twofold nature. There is the physical race with its different types—the Caucasian, the Oriental, the Negroid and so on. Then there is the spiritual race, the consciousness archetype that a given wave of life is intended to make manifest.

These are called, esoterically, root races. They do have

---

* I am not yet in any way discussing the propagation of more forms for incoming souls. I am discussing the release of an energy of synthesis between two people which can then be used to build with.

physical manifestations. A certain physical type will be more characterlstlc of Its consclousness expresslon than another physlcal lype. But it is important to understand that a root race is not limited to physical bodies. What is called the fifth root race, the present dominant consciousness expression, which is the race of mental development, occupies every known body. A fifth root race individual can be Caucasian, can be Negroid, can be Oriental. It is fundamentally a matter of consciousness.

The development of these races is to create a collective body—a body composed of literally millions of individual units which all taken together will fulfil within the body of the Earth as a whole a particular kind of manifestation.

The fifth root race is designed to manifest mind. This means that some kind of control must be exercised over the development of the race, both its conscious development and its form development. In the early days of man's evolution this development was exercised by beings who were illumined beings, master beings, who were the prototypes of given races. They exercised a great deal of control over what souls were attracted from the inner planes to take incarnation through the race, and also the kind of bodies that were created.

Many ancient cultures had programmes of selective breeding, planned genetics, but whether this programme existed or not there was a necessity to protect the incoming soul from what is a mixture of vibrations. For when sexual intercourse takes place and the male joins his sperm with the egg in the female, the sexual union that creates a body for an incoming soul really is taking place on other levels as well. There is the etheric union, probably astral or feeling union, possibly mental and in some cases spiritual union. The parents are supplying more than just physical energy to create the birth vortex, and the soul enters.

Once conception takes place—the soul is linked with its developing body from the moment of conception even though it does not enter that body for several months after conception—then the soul with the help of forces on the inner planes begins to build its subtle vehicles: its mental body, its emotional body, its etheric body. All of these are building within the womb and about the womb of the mother at the same time as the physical body is developing as an embryo. ·

The thing that had to be guarded against was promiscuity during pregnancy, particularly the early stages—promiscuity within the energy field that the parents were building up, which was designed to create what could really be called a home—a home in the occult sense, which means a field of thought, of emotion, of physical surrounding which lasts for several years and provides a stable environment—a certain kind of energy environment through which the soul can develop, because truly the soul is building its vehicles for a period of several years after birth takes place.

So marriage was instituted—this is the second reason for its institution—to protect the integrity of the incoming vibrations of the soul and to channel the sexual energy of man into definite areas of building so that what was created was what the guardians of the race wanted to be created.

In the early days marriage between races was prohibited for the reason of keeping a purity of vibration and consciousness within the races. This pattern is no longer true because the races that are developing in our future are no longer races of form but races of consciousness. It is quite likely that intermarriage—carried out with wisdom and balance and understanding that it is more than just bodies interrelating but also cultures interrelating when you have intermarriage—will become increasingly common as we prepare for the universal races of the future.

In the past marriage was instituted for these two reasons: the ceremony itself to be an initiation in which definite energies were invoked for the blessing of the couple and to give them a head start in the unifying of their energy fields, and as a sacred institution in order that the vibrational pattern of creativity between the couples was kept concentrated.

Creation takes place through concentration of energy, not through dispersal of energy. The marriage laws pertaining to adultery and promiscuity are often expressed in negative fashion: do not do this and do not do that or you will be punished.

But behind these laws lies a certain fundamental truth. When the race was young it had to learn through law. As man grows in wisdom he can learn and act through his own inner divinity, and then a different kind of morality takes over—the morality of the soul and of the higher love and higher wisdom. But initially there was instituted for the race definite laws concerning the sanctity of the marriage bond simply because man has to learn how to harness his creative forces with purposeful intent and consecration. (Consecration is simply another way of saying concentration, a rhythm that moves towards one purpose and does not disperse itself.)

Marriage is an adventure in consciousness. It is the coming together of two separated beings to reveal the truth that in fact they are one being, and to harness their unique energies in such a way that they do not lose their uniqueness, but a third force, a third factor which I will call illumination can be released.

It is a challenge to learn to integrate oneself with oneself. It is equally a challenge to learn how to integrate oneself with others: the challenge of communication, of love, of communion.

It is not a challenge that is met very swiftly. It is not a work that can be accomplished very quickly. So the release of this third energy, which I am calling illumination or blessing, is not something which is released overnight. It is certainly not released through the marriage ceremony itself. It is released through a process of the two individuals learning how to increasingly synthesize themselves, how to blend their emotional levels and their mental levels, how to blend any one level of consciousness with all the levels of the partner as best you can—and then to go beyond your best and do it better.

It is an adventure in divinity. It is exploring the nature of one's divinity, one's ability to create something and to release that vital energy of illumination.

Sex plays an important part in this, for this is a sexual pattern in its initial stages on all levels. It is attraction. It has to be some kind of attraction to bring you together. Then it is the work of union. Physical sex, physical mating takes place very quickly. This is not true of mating on the higher levels. It is not true of learning how to mate emotionally. It is not true of learning how to mate mentally. These take time. It takes intent, a desire to accomplish this. It takes a love.

Attraction, union, synthesis can take place very rapidly on the physical levels. Creation physically can take place very rapidly there too unless the couple has been careful. But this is not true on emotional and mental levels—not the kind of creativity which is the release of an energy which is not only potent, powerful in its blessing but also long lasting in its effect.

Two people can come together, male and female. They can have a good time together. They can play a game of chess together, they can go out and enjoy a movie together, they can go to a dance together, they can have some kind of pleasure and union, mentally, emotionally—and something is created.

Two people come together and work out a song or a dance or a play, but that relationship will tend to dissipate if it has only been a momentary thing, an acquaintance. But if these two or three or four or whatever number work together consistently, they build up a team consciousness, and what is released through this blending is an energy that not only is highly creative and potent but also very long lasting in its effects.

It is cumulative so that after a while two people who have achieved that union can come together and immediately the sparks start flying, creativity starts to pour.

You may experience this in a given life, in this life, with people whom you have never met before. But if you are experiencing it, it is because somewhere along the line, in some life or other, you have already established that powerful link.

The great challenge of man is that he has not learned yet how to consecrate himself; therefore he has not learned how to purify himself, how to harness his energies towards accomplishing one thing at a time. Man, speaking generally—this is true for most people at some point or other—tends to be pulled physically, emotionally or mentally to a number of different things and so energies get scattered.

The function of marriage conceived by the guardians of the race is to harness that within an auric field, a sphere of energy, so that man learns how to concentrate on at least one thing in his life, and that is achieving union with another person. If he can do that, really achieve it, then he has released for himself a tremendous energy of upliftment in his spiritual evolution.

Celibacy is one way that many people in the past and people now are attempting to unfold spiritually. The marriage bond and the responsibilities thereof is another way. It is fundamentally a sounder way. Ultimately everyone must experience in one life or another the responsibilities of marriage.

An interesting book which was written through telepathic transmission by a very reliable sensitive detailed the experiences of a man who refused to marry in one life, and found that upon leaving his physical body one of the things he had to do was to enter into what could be called an astral marriage—the taking up of a partnership with another individual on the emotional realm just to learn the discipline of how to blend himself in the giving of himself to another person emotionally and mentally.

I am not suggesting by this that everyone who is not married or does not wish to marry must at some point, whether in this life or after death, get married. What I am suggesting is that at some point in your life pattern, at some point in your history as a soul, the experiences and discipline of marriage must become part of your experience. I say this because the purposes of celibacy are to harness the creative energy for a given task as specified by the soul, or to give the person a discipline of absolute control over the physical and emotional nature. At some point everyone has to learn how to have that control.

In marriage a much vaster field of experience is offered, and in the creation and liberation of this energy of illumination the true birth channel is created. The souls of the future will be brought through what can be best described as immaculate birth—which simply means birth created through absolute purity of being: two beings uniting sexually, physically. Undoubtedly the race has a long way to go before it can propagate itself through other means: uniting mentally, emotionally, spiritually; uniting with full motive, full understanding, all the levels of the being moving into that union for both people; a blending releasing this channel of illumination, of spiritual intent. Through this the soul enters and from this energy builds its vehicles and takes its physical form.

A child born out of purity has a head start in life. A child born out of less than that has to overcome the mixed vibrations of the inharmonious or unresolved vibrations which were present in the parents' consciousness during conception and during pregnancy and during the developmental years in the home.

For this reason it will probably remain true as a guide for the race that the ideal—no longer quite the law—but certainly the vision that is promoted is that the sexual function physically will be held within the marriage.

The reason for this is simple. In the wielding of energy of a creative nature man has to learn how to focus it to accomplish a given task before he is released to accomplish other tasks. A person who takes on the challenge of being an instrument through which souls can enter must also take on the responsibility, ideally, of providing the greatest channel through which such souls can enter, providing the most harmonious and stable environment that it is possible to create. This means that energy cannot be dissipated. Bonds which would pull energy out of the marriage must be carefully balanced.

The use of sexual energy is one way of establishing bonds with individuals. It establishes a definite etheric bond which will dissipate itself in time, but it can establish emotional and mental bonds as well. If these are established from higher levels, from the level of the soul, through the principles of self-law and governing, that is something else again.

We can always rationalize and say, 'Well, it was my soul that was directing me in any given action.' But ultimately we are our own tribunal. We are the product of our creativity. And if we rationalize too much we are going to end up with not a very good product. A judge once said, 'A lawyer who has himself for his client has a fool for a lawyer.' So a creator who plays fast and loose with his creative power without being honest with himself and knowing what he is doing has only a fool for a god.

There is a necessity for man to learn how to use the energies of his consciousness to build within marriage, within a relationship between two people, that kind of rhythm which creates a total sexual harmony, not just physical but emotional and mental and spiritual, that lasts, releasing an energy that lasts, that is relatively permanent and able to nourish the developing soul patterns, the souls of the parent, the souls of the children, so that they truly grow into the full potential that a human being is capable of. That is what we are after.

Some people say that sex should only be used for the purposes of propagation. My understanding of this is quite different. Sex should indeed be used and harnessed for propagation, but we see this in a broader sense of the term than simply the creation of physical bodies. The physical union between two people in marriage often starts out with not being very satisfactory. There is a great deal of blending that needs to take place, and it is this blending, this relationship between the couple, that should be dealt with.

Sex physically is one of the greatest tools that man has for the exchange and circulation of energy and for intimacy and the giving of oneself and the opening of oneself in trust and in love and in patience and in caring to help establish this communion, this synthesis between people. Sex should be used as the beautiful tool for synthesis which it is.

I certainly believe that the training centres for new age consciousness that are developing, the centres of the future, will have sex education as a fundamental part of the curriculum, planned parenthood in the sense of training people how to be parents—something that western culture is greatly lacking; how to understand the principles of soul development, of physical development, of emotional development, of mental development, so that the task of parenthood can be discharged, not as a duty but as a fantastic creative adventure, a partnership with the incoming souls to create something so splendid, so beautiful— things that the world has never seen; and the ability of a couple to blend sexually, not out of duty, not out of obligation, not out of a sense of propagating the race, but because that is a means of communicating together—that is important; how to make that blending as perfect as possible and then how to pass from that blending to higher blendings until you have the immaculate marriage being created.

It is a challenge in communication and creativity. Many people are saying now that the problem with marriage is that it has become too restrictive, and this is true. We have lost the understanding of what marriage is. It has become ritualistic. It has

74

become legalistic, part of our social structure designed to protect the woman in most cases from the advantage which a man can take of a woman in economic and legal ways.

But if this is the only way in which marriage is seen, simply on a materialistic, economic, social, legal level, or fulfilling some law that some God has given without an understanding of why the law is there and what that God is and where he lives and where his temple is within oneself, then it is no wonder that marriage is under attack. It is the same reason that God is under attack. The best thing that ever happened was when Christian theologians said that God is dead because it created a controversy that caused people to begin to re-evaluate: just who is God? What do we mean by divinity?

That is part of the new age adventure: to begin to understand our Beloved in such a way that we can achieve marriage with him, union with our own divinity.

The challenge to marriage is of a similar nature. It may be very good for the institution of marriage as we know it to be destroyed so that it can be replaced by its true purpose, which will probably be very similar in some ways to what we already have.

One of the criticisms being levelled against marriage is that it is too exclusive. 'How can one person be expected to fulfil the needs of one other person for a lifetime? It is ridiculous. What we really need is a group so that one person can have his or her needs fulfilled by many people and can in turn fulfil the needs of a number of people.'

There is a great deal of truth in this because when we operate on the level of our personalities we tend to operate just as fragments, as limited beings: 'this is my personality structure and there are certain things I will express and other things I will not express.' Obviously there are going to be people—and if I were married probably my mate would be one—who would have needs that I was not allowing to be met through the personality identity that I was conceiving for myself.

But I wish you to understand that the challenge here is not one of marriage; it is not one of two people not being able to meet each other's needs. It is again the challenge of identity. There is something very wrong in that concept, and what is wrong about it is that it is saying that other people must meet our needs, when the whole crux of the challenge of identity is to realize that the only place our needs are ever fulfilled in any lasting way is from the divinity that is within us. Another person can help reveal that divinity to us, like a signpost pointing to our destination, but we have to tap it. We have to do the work, to go in and release it and demonstrate it.

It is the basic principle that Jesus taught: 'Seek ye first the kingdom of heaven—or the kingdom of wholeness—and all your needs are met.' It is a fundamental precept for the law of manifestation. Just as we do not look at Findhorn to individuals to supply our needs, it is the same thing in marriage. If you want a perfect marriage do not look to your mate to supply your needs. That is not why you got married. Look to God. Look to the divinity within, and use marriage for what it is intended to be: as an adventure in joy and balance, in love and wisdom, to reveal that divinity through your mutual interactions, and through the demonstration you can provide of the resolution of duality and the manifestation of wholeness.

In this way the path of the householder, the path of marriage, becomes a path to the divine; and more than that, it becomes a path to a renewed world. Marriage properly utilized is a key, a gateway, through which a whole new energy of incoming soul life can find access to the planet, and can develop, and grace the world with the manifestation of a new race.

As man grows he will increasingly step free of external law, of morality, of ethics as applied from outside himself. He will increasingly come under the rhythm and direction of his highest nature and in this he will find a freedom which he has only dreamed of until now. He will begin to rediscover—those who have lost it—the significance and purpose of marriage. He will also begin to understand the greater rhythms of marriage—the rhythms that bind us together in groups and in communities, the marriage with God, the marriage with humanity.

The next chapter will deal with this group blending, the group marriage, the soul marriage, the divine marriage. But before it can be expanded into a greater form we must learn to touch and to recognize and to know the source from which that expansion takes place—the soul.

Marriage between two people is truly a God-given way in which this touching can take place, this recognition can take place, this unfoldment can take place. It is not the only path, certainly. People who choose to remain alone but to find their blending and express their divinity in other ways can find the same touching in these other ways.

But for marriage we stand at a time when those who serve the race have an opportunity to demonstrate again the fulfilment that it offers and to see marriage not as a bond, not as a limitation, not as the old joke says—the ball and chain. A person only feels limited when he has lost interest and has lost the flow of energy and of creative vitalization that was there in the first place. We think of being married to one person for many years, and at times that seems a horrible concept. It does seem rather limiting. But it is only limiting when viewed from the level of personality, in thinking in terms of time, thinking in terms of need, thinking in terms of limitation.

If you understand that in marriage as in any relationship you are exploring the reality of the soul and its basic communion and the adventure of communication, then you have to know that you are engaged in the most exciting adventure that a human being can enter upon. That is where the interest, and more than just interest, the intensity of excitement can enter in.

There is no reason at all for the passion, the romance, the splendour of a marriage to disappear after the first few weeks or months or years. If it does, it is because marriage was only entered into from personality levels, and then sufficient work was not done to lift it beyond those levels.

It can be kept alive, burning in greater and greater splendour as it lifts the person out of time into timelessness, and demonstrates that in truth the love that was felt and that prompted the coming together in the marriage in the first place was simply the opening of a door upon a reality of oneness that is there for us each.

The Group Consciousness

I want here to review the various themes of this book. I began with purity which was defined as being that state of consciousness and of being in which all of an individual's different levels of functioning are working together in a harmonious and cooperative fashion. They are integrated. They are united in synthesis and a person is enabled thereby to have a clear picture of where he is, of who he is, of where he is going, and of why he is behaving the way he is.

Impurity was defined as the functioning of an individual who is acting through unclear motivations, several levels of consciousness reacting to his environment and promoting actions of various kinds but not coordinated action, not clear or honest action.

Each of the levels of man which operate within form tend to seek outside forms, outside experiences, external stimuli to form the basis for identity, for defining who I am, for answering the question, 'Who am I?' The soul we defined as being that level which transcends form as we know it and operates from the inside out. It does not say 'I am that' and then determine whatever 'that' may be: 'I am that body, I am that man, I am that set of past experiences.' The soul simply says 'I am that I am.' It is the source of our identity.

A person who is in contact with his soul, with his divine level, is not a person who is seeking in his environment for answers to the question, 'Who am I?' Therefore he can approach his environment with a good deal more peace and stability. The amount of that peace and stability and purity of action depends on the extent to which the individual is attuned to his higher nature.

Our discussions then entered into the realm of energy and how we draw to ourselves vitalizing energy which we use to build our various bodies and also to build our sense of identity.

The most all-pervasive and powerful of these energies is the one which, as it expresses physically, we term sexual energy. This is the energy of attraction, of union and synthesis, and of opening the portals for that vital energy of creativity to flow. It is the energy of creation.

In our discussions of sexual energy, of morality, the right use of sex and human relations, we have concentrated upon how this reflects upon our knowledge of who we are; how it builds for us a purified body of expression by helping us to attune to inner sources of strength, of peace, of awareness, of identity, and to draw all the various impulses of bodily instinct, of emotion and desire, of intellect and mentality into this centre so that all of the energies of the lower forms are governed by the consciousness of the soul.

The last chapter was about marriage. There are many things that could be said about marriage, but what we are interested in is: what role does marriage play as an arena within which the energies of creativity and of building have expression and release?

We first defined marriage as being the state of synthesis and creativity existing between two or more levels, between two polarities. The first marriage that each of us experiences is that blending of energy which makes possible the coherent functioning of our various bodies: our physical body, our vital or etheric body, our emotional body, our mental body, and our soul.

The second level of marriage which we experience is one instituted ages and ages ago in which man would duplicate in his human experience the drama of the union of the polarities which is one of the basic creative principles on which this universe is founded. He would do this by learning not only how to synthesize and unite the various levels of his own being so that he could become a purified and illumined being, but how at the same time to unify and unite himself with the levels of another person. In other words, how could two people assist each other to create an atmosphere and environment of steadily and continuously unfolding harmony and oneness, so that man's identity which is part of the God-self, the one-self, could be revealed?

In approaching marriage from this standpoint I have not attempted to consider marriage in its legal forms nor even that much in its social forms as it is expressed by various cultures. Ultimately within the present experience pattern of the human race monogamy is the only form of marriage that man can experience, simply because even if you have several wives or several husbands you can only relate to one of them at a time.

The group relationships that we are involved in are essentially patterns formed out of a number of individual pair-bonds, which may be quite casual but none the less represent a basic polar manifestation, male-female in fashion. This is true even if it is two men or two women. In any given creative relationship someone is going to be acting as the initiator of energy, someone else is going to be acting as the negative pole, the receiver of energy. Between the two the third force, the force of creative illumination, can be made manifest.

But man as he approaches the threshold of knowing his soul, of really experiencing his divine self—not just being told about it, not just reading about it, but actually experiencing it—also approaches the threshold of true group consciousness.

81

For the first time in fairly recent human history since man became more enmeshed in a consciousness of form and polarity and duality and division and separation, man is at a point where he can begin to comprehend what a true group expression, a group marriage, could be like.

Marriage as a modern institution is under severe questioning. It is right that this is so because it is necessary that we evaluate patterns which have become simply traditional and see what is the reality, the livingness which was originally within them, which all of our institutions are ultimately designed to embody.

An institution of any kind grows out of a need and out of some kind of revelation and is designed to embody a truth. As time goes on the need may change. The truth may become forgotten as the institution becomes itself its own reason for being. At that point the institution becomes an illusion. It becomes a barrier to the realization of reality.

Many people today are struggling with the concept of marriage simply because they are struggling with the illusion of marriage, with the social and legal concept and the romantic concept and not with the actual reality of a given relationship.

Marriage is designed to express a certain reality of relationship, something deeper than a simple casual acquaintancy, something deeper than purely working together, something that involves a level of giving, a level of sharing, a level of commitment and responsibility, an intimacy which potentially can result in two things: the annihilation of both individuals on the one hand through a sheer act of giving, and the resurrection of both individuals on the other hand through a discovery of a greater identity born through the process of this giving, through the process of sharing, through the process of loving.

Whether or not any given marriage between two people should stay in existence, or what the patterns within that marriage should be, will increasingly as man develops be determined by the individual's ability to perceive the reality of what they are creating together—if the marriage is a state in which they are learning how to express themselves in a godly fashion, how to create with another person.

The ideal still to be held before mankind is the sanctity of the marriage. This is not to be interpreted in terms of not being aware of the reality of energy flows between individuals, and of certain karmic bonds which can exist and which can then dissolve. Two people who have been brought together through such a bond, or through energy patterns that have fulfilled their purpose, may find that now in the divine scheme of things it is right for them to separate.

Law, whether it is moral law or the prescriptive laws which our legislatures give to us, is designed to help man until such time as he can tap the source of his own self-governing principles, his soul, which is at one with the rhythm of law which we call the will of God, divine law. Jesus said this so aptly when he was asked what was the greatest commandment of the ten that Moses gave, the Hebraic law. He said: 'The greatest commandment is to love God with all your strength and to love your neighbour as yourself.' If you obey that law you fulfil all of the others. Within the soul is that awareness, that ability of consciousness, of group awareness which when realized will fulfil the essence of all human laws, legalistic, moralistic.

What is this consciousness that we are approaching and which many people are beginning to tap? The soul is not only the source of identity, it is also the heart, the essence behind marriage. It is the real pulse of which all human relationships are intended to be the circulatory system, the revelatory system. For the soul knows that it is one with all life. It knows this not in any kind of self-abnegation, self-denial, but in self-affirmation. The soul lives knowing that it is one with the ocean of life. Hence it knows, it experiences, its oneness with others.

This is not the same thing as saying that it experiences the flow of energy with others that is brought about through work. It is not the same thing as saying that my soul and the soul of Mr. X, because we are one in realization, are necessarily one in function, or in manifestation, or in form. Mr. X may be incarnating on Earth to manifest an energy quite distinctly different from what I am manifesting. We may work on opposite sides of the Earth and there may be no real contact between us and no necessity for contact. In fact contact between us could conceivably be harmful on a form level. But that does not make any difference to our ability to realize that we are harmonious parts of a single whole.

Hence our ability to work together, fulfilling our given missions, functions in harmony. For example, the cells of my liver and the cells of my eye and the cells of my heart are all performing different functions. If they get intermixed I am in trouble physically. It is not right for the cells of one part of the body to attempt to take over the cells of another part. But it is still necessary for them to know that they are functioning as part of a wholeness.

The soul is, for humanity, for each individual, that level of consciousness that permits us to have that awareness. We then have to translate that awareness into some kind of practical action, practical revelation.

The soul opens the door for creativity because the soul does not present blocks to creativity. The soul does not say 'I cannot do that,' or 'I refuse to work with so-and-so,' or 'I refuse to do a certain kind of task.' The soul is perfectly aware of what it can do. It is aware as well of what it should not do in any given pattern of timing and function. It is also aware of the people with whom it should work.

Out of this awareness grows the energy which can form for man the foundations of a new social pattern—a social pattern that will be exemplified by a group consciousness in the same way that our present social pattern has been characterized by individual consciousness. We are an individualistic society, or we have been. What does this mean in terms of a person's identity and the use of various energies, particularly sexual energy, in revealing who he is as a creator? Man, in spite of different marriage patterns— polygamy, polyandry—has never really experienced in any large scale measure true group marriage simply because he has never experienced group consciousness on any wide scale. He has never experienced the consciousness of the soul acting through form, actually brought down and manifesting through a physical body, bringing the divine into incarnated life.

The true pattern of group marriage is not built upon people living together, or people having sex together, or people supporting each other emotionally and mentally and fulfilling each other's needs on these levels. That is simply coming together. That is the same thing as putting all of us into one room. We are all in one place but we do not have a group consciousness. We have an intermingling of auras. The auras of some people are not compatible with the auras of others. As a consequence there are certain patterns of tension, certain patterns of separation, certain patterns of division, which a sensitive person can be aware of. That is quite common on the levels of form.

To create group consciousness means that we are acting from the source of that consciousness, from the level of the soul. It is pulling it down and creating the channels through which it can flow.

Let me give you an example of what I mean by this, a form of yoga. If you have a clogged drain you can keep pumping things into it in the hope that you are going to force through whatever is blocking it. Or you can operate from the other end to open the channel and allow that which is blocking to move through, releasing the pressure, releasing the blockage.

God is pressure acting upon us. From our soul is a continuous

85

pouring of energy down. We on the other hand are continually looking up, looking to heaven, through prayer, through aspiration, for the answer of need, the answer of desire. But this creates a blockage because it is the equivalent of our talking to God at the same time he is talking to us. As a consequence no one is hearing anything.

Our way of revealing group consciousness is through the relationships that we have, the actions that we manifest, the work that we do, being themselves consecrated to revealing what we understand as the life and rhythm of the soul. This is exactly what Jesus said: 'I will love God with all my strength and I will love my neighbour as myself.' I will translate love into a practical form—a form of service, a form of awareness, a form of giving, a form of communication. As I learn to communicate with people, as I learn to give to people, to be aware of people in a wise and balanced way, for myself, for my environment, then energy begins to flow.

Throughout the world, under the impact of the need to develop group consciousness, people are starting to come together to attempt to create group consciousness from the bottom up as it were. It is as if a number of people came together in a large house in order to live together. As a result of living there, communally or how ever, they would hope to create a group consciousness.

Now that might be so. If they can stick it out long enough then perhaps eventually they would create a group consciousness. It can be done from the bottom up. But the chances are far more likely that long before they reach a point where they have begun to contact the soul and bring it through in a group fashion, they will have splintered themselves through the sandpapering and the friction on personality levels.

The way to create a group consciousness is by individually beginning to realize one's divine identity, one's soul. You are a group consciousness. You are the group consciousness. The group consciousness is not made up of people. It is made of a state of being.

Likewise a group marriage—which is nothing more than a group consciousness that is acting in a highly creative way, revealing energy, bringing energy down and giving it form—is a state of being. It is not a collection of people. I, all by myself, am a group marriage as the various levels of my being come together and work in harmony. When I work creatively with someone else we are a group marriage. There are several levels operating between us to permit a creative flow. It is a state of consciousness and it is best approached in that fashion.

Likewise sex is a state of consciousness. We think of sex as being an action, an energy, a relationship. But any doctor or psychologist or marriage counsellor who has any understanding of human nature realizes that sex is not a physical manifestation as much as it is a mental one. Sex exists in the brain and so do a lot of other things that we experience. We are creatures of thought. We are states of consciousness manifesting outwards, revealing ourselves.

In the concept and the awareness of one's sexual nature and of one's link with others through that nature it is important that we expand these concepts beyond their physical counterparts and reflections and see that we are dealing with states of being, states of consciousness, which are either open to life in a trusting, loving, clear, pure, balanced way, or one is closed to life.

Jesus, manifesting the Christ, the energy of cosmic consciousness, oceanic consciousness, oneness with the whole, manifested the most sexually complete and powerful being to have walked this Earth, simply because he allowed nothing of the personality nature to interfere with his ability to achieve union, synthesis, and creativity with all of life—with people, with plants, with earth, with sky, with dimensions beyond our knowing. He was one with that and out of that oneness was created a revelation of light, of love, of wisdom. He became a seed point for a great group marriage.

And the Christian church speaks of itself theologically in terms of being a group marriage, with Christ being the bridegroom and the church being the bride, with all the nuns and the priests uniting with Jesus, becoming part of his consciousness, extensions of his being, and with the whole church becoming mystically the body of Christ.

Rather than group marriage I prefer to use the term group consciousness because it is really what we are dealing with. The marriage concept is still very much encrusted with legal, social, sexual connotations. Because we have the kind of culture we do, marriage is still seen as being that state in which a person can legally and correctly experience sexual relationships.

But *that,* I wish you to see, is a vastly restricting definition, both of marriage and of sex. It also limits one's identity of oneself as a sexual being, as a living being, as a creating being, as a loving and relating being.

As we begin to touch the level of our soul and to draw on its awareness we will begin to have the rich and really tremendous experience of suddenly knowing people, perhaps people you have only met just moments ago, as part of you. What they are physically does not make much difference. What they are as personalities does not make much difference. You simply know that in the course of divine events you and that other individual are one. You have a function to perform together even if you may be physically quite separate.

You begin to be aware that you walk through life not alone but as part of a group. Each of us is part of a group—an ever expanding group!

One of the great joys of unfoldment is to begin to recognize that this is so and to begin to identify people with whom you share these links. Out of this awareness will undoubtedly grow, as our New Age develops and the society that springs from it develops, a pattern which will revolve around what will appear to be on the outside the equivalent of the old extended family or the tribe, but now functioning as an entirely different organism—no longer simply a group of people banding together because of economic physical necessity, or emotional or mental necessity, or even simply because of blood ties, but a group of people who begin functioning in harmonious rhythm together, even though they may be quite different and perhaps quite incompatible on personality levels, because they share a unifying flow that is coming from the level of the soul. Call them what you will—affinity groups, soul groups, group marriages.

What does this do in terms of practical everyday morality? Let us realize that the evolution of the race is for man to learn not how to obey the law but how to *be* the law. There is a vast, vast difference. If you *are* the law it means that you are at one with the whole. For divine law simply exists. It is not a prescription. It is not a legislature of angels sitting up there debating for several centuries and then passing a law. It describes qualities and characteristics that are part of the very structure of the universe.

We talk about the law of gravity, the law of thermodynamics, and the divine laws are like that. If you are part of that, one with such a law, that simply means that you understand and share as the very rhythm of your being the quality and reason and importance of that given structure, that given foundation on which the universe is built. You realize that it is the same law. It is the manifestation of that law that enables you to function.

Sex is a law like that. Sex is a natural law. We have encompassed it with a lot of man-made laws but it is basically a divine law and as such it is integrally part of the balanced and harmonious manifestation of the universe, at least on the levels with which we are dealing. The original revelation of various moral codes in ancient days was to try and get man to approximate as closely as possible those energy flows which create the greatest

89

harmony within the universe, laws governing the relationship of separate units.

The basis of this law is the law of synthesis, that one plus one does not equal two. In God's arithmetic one plus one equals three because the sum is greater, the whole is greater than the sum of its parts. I and another individual working together in a truly synthetic or complementary relationship, giving relationship, create something that is more than just the two of us being together. We reveal the wholeness.

Sex on all the levels in which it manifests is simply a subdivision of the law of attraction and of synthesis that permits the wholeness to be revealed.

As we become attuned to that, at one with it, through our own inner being, we begin to understand how the use of the energies of attraction, of synthesis, go to make up who we are, go to make up the environment in which we experience our world, and in a larger sense contribute to the total flow of the divine scheme of things.

Man has grasped this principle and expressed it in folksy terms, as when he says 'Birds of a feather flock together' or 'You can judge a man by his friends.' This is not always so. Many people criticized Jesus because most of his friends were from the lower levels of society, or they were horrible creatures like tax collectors, or they were prostitutes or drunkards or gluttons. But it is a true enough statement that the relationships a person forms, the energy that he puts into a relationship is a two-way thing and acts upon his own image of himself and his own creativity as he is constantly building his self-image.

All forms of union—sexual union, mental or emotional union, soul union—create an energy link. It will last for however long it is still being vitalized from some level. These links form vast and intricate webs between us and are constantly shifting on the personality levels. But what we are, what we think we are, is often built from the energy that comes to us from these links.

The misuse of this kind of understanding is the person who says, 'I will not associate with certain people because they are bad for me spiritually.' A sort of spiritual snobbery. 'I do not want my vibrations mixed up with so-and-so.' If a person knows the purity that one is and is attuned to one's soul, no one is going to 'impure' you. That can only be done from within.

The point I wish to communicate here is that the energy that we send out from us, the choices we make, the relationships we create through our choices, have a direct effect upon the building of our own being and our own self-image and our own sense of identity. It has therefore a direct bearing on how we conceive of ourselves, how we will express ourselves.

When a person understands this, when he begins to have that attunement, when he is the law, he is not going to act in any way that will disturb or distort the true balance or the true wholeness. He may definitely act in ways that disrupt human-conceived wholeness, or that disrupt crystallized patterns on personality levels, but he will do it with knowing and not necessarily through impulse or through purely destructive motive.

In that kind of consciousness morality on human levels is replaced by morality on a soul level, a super-morality, a morality based on giving, on selflessness, on awareness of the whole, on love. Out of that can be born group manifestations, group patterns, which however they express, whatever kind of relationships, physical, emotional, mental, are formed, will only serve to benefit the whole.

We enter an age when traditional patterns are undergoing transformation. In that transformation during this interim period it is like living in a vast laboratory in which we are attempting to experiment and see what is the best pattern to carry us into the future.

Much of this experimentation is taking place by people who

know there is something there to be brought through but they do not know what it is, and the only way they have of approaching it is through what they are accustomed to—through physical levels, through emotional levels, through mental levels.

Those who would serve the race and bring down into demonstration the ideas, the powerful images which will uplift the race and carry it into the new, must be able to demonstrate that there are other levels at work, that we can move fearlessly into a new age and know that if we are moving step by step in attunement with our soul level we are not going to create chaos or imbalance. We are going to be able to heal the chaos and imbalance which we may encounter. We can demonstrate higher meanings to love, to marriage, to all forms of human relationship in such a way that the society of which we are a part can share in that revelation and use it to mould for itself new pathways into its destiny, into its future.

Purity, identity, attunement, love, responsibility, awareness, caring, communication—all of these words represent qualities, states of mind and states of being, attitudes of action and approach to life, which can make us revealers of man's unfolding heritage and revealers of the next stage in human evolution, the revelation of group consciousness, the revelation of the true group marriage in which we learn how to blend together, to work together, to create as one.

The community (Findhorn) is already an expression of a group marriage in that it is a group of people, very diverse personalities, yet still to a signficant degree blending themselves and creating through that blending. The community is not created through people living together, through people necessarily working together. It is created through people learning to attune to what they are within themselves and through that attunement to discover their true relationships with each other, and through that discovery to build the foundations for the future.

Marriage is a vast subject which involves much more than I

have attempted to go into in this small book. I have not really been interested in trying to define what constitutes the pathways for balanced relationships between two people or between groups of people.

What I am interested in is to communicate this idea:

We are each of us creators, each of us divine. We are on a quest to discover that identity and to know it;

Relationships that we form with people are one way in which we reveal this identity because the universe itself is based on relationship;

God is in one sense revealed through relationship. He *is* relationship at work;

Sex is a basic foundation energy that lies at the heart of all relationships;

Marriage is the sanctified use of relationship to reveal divinity and creativity. (By sanctified I mean that you know what you are doing and you are doing it consciously with commitment to this creativity.)

Marriage is a state of consciousness, of blending through that consciousness. Through the relationships, the links that we form, the energy that we express, we either build for ourselves the revelation of our identity or in some way we obscure it. The choice is ours.

For people who move into the new age the choice had best be theirs, because the new age is an age where there is needed that group of people who through attunement can be self-governing, act as the law, as the divine, as the right, as the love.

This is a continuous call of these days and each of you are responding in some way or another, or will begin to respond. The initiate, the disciple, the follower of the light in all ages has generally been a person who stands free in consciousness from the culture of which he is a part and yet he blends into that culture and works with its energies unless he is specifically directed from

93

other levels, from his own inner wisdom, to do otherwise.

Therefore I am not interested in ways in which our various institutions such as marriage will change, for they will change as we undergo transformation in consciousness and become forces of greater awareness within our society. Then we will reveal marriage and love as they exist in the reality of our relationships and that will be a transforming power released upon our Earth.

As you seek this attunement and seek to work within it, always be aware of the culture and of the people within which you are moving and with whom you are working. Learn how to be not only a revealer but a communicator to the best extent possible.

Learn how to take the best of the culture as a bridge to work with those who cannot move to your state of interest, of attunement, or of swift movement into self-transformation; but at the same time move yourselves and be aware of the identity that seeks to live within you.

OTHER BOOKS FROM FINDHORN

These titles are available from:
Findhorn Publications
The Park
Forres IV36 OTZ
Scotland
or write for complete book and tape catalogues.